DEVIL'S ADVOCATES

T0341949

DEVIL'S ADVOCATES is a series of books devoted to exploring the classics of horror cinema. Contributors to the series come from the fields of teaching, academia, journalism and fiction, but all have one thing in common: a passion for the horror film and a desire to share it with the widest possible audience.

'The admirable Devil's Advocates series is not only essential – and fun – reading for the serious horror fan but should be set texts on any genre course.'
Dr Ian Hunter, Reader in Film Studies, De Montfort University, Leicester

'Auteur Publishing's new Devil's Advocates critiques on individual titles... offer bracingly fresh perspectives from passionate writers. The series will perfectly complement the BFI archive volumes.' **Christopher Fowler,** *Independent on Sunday*

'Devil's Advocates has proven itself more than capable of producing impassioned, intelligent analyses of genre cinema... quickly becoming the go-to guys for intelligent, easily digestible film criticism.' *Horror Talk.com*

'Auteur Publishing continue the good work of giving serious critical attention to significant horror films.' *Black Static*

 DevilsAdvocatesbooks

DevilsAdBooks

Devil's Advocates

SUSPIRIA

Alexandra Heller-Nicholas

Acknowledgments

This book is indebted to two people: Dario Argento for obvious reasons; and John Atkinson from Auteur for kindly allowing me the opportunity to join the fantastic Devil's Advocates series. My gratitude to fellow DA author Neil Mitchell for his ongoing support, and thanks to a number of others: Dean Brandum, Shaun Cola, Michael Delsol, Fiona Drury, Rachel Fensham, Lee Gambin, Ian Gouldstone, James Gracey, Jade Henshaw, Stacy Livitsanis, Anne Marsh, Angela Ndalianis, Eloise Roberts, David Surman, Yuka Takashima, Mark Tansley and Valentina Maxwell Tansley, Banana Yoshimoto, and Matias Viegener. Thanks also for my co-hosts at Triple R radio in Melbourne on the Plato's Cave film criticism programme (Cerise Howard, Josh Nelson and Thomas Caldwell), and to my fellow editors at SensesOfCinema.com. I particularly wish to thank cinematographer Luciano Tovoli who spent a great deal of time talking to me about his work on the film. And finally, thanks of course to my family, especially my husband Christian.

This book is dedicated to Casper, my very own work of art.

First published in 2015 by
Auteur, 24 Hartwell Crescent, Leighton Buzzard LU7 1NP
www.auteur.co.uk
Copyright © Auteur 2015

Series design: Nikki Hamlett at Cassels Design
Set by Cassels Design www.casselsdesign.co.uk
Printed and bound by CPI Group (UK) Ltd, Croydon, CR0 4YY

British Library Cataloguing-in-Publication Data
A catalogue record for this book is available from the British Library

ISBN paperback: 978-09932384-7-5
ISBN ebook: 978-09932384-8-2

CONTENTS

Suspiria *poster painted by Shaun Cola*

INTRODUCTION: THE SECRET OF THE IRISES

As one of the most globally recognisable instances of twentieth-century Eurohorror, Dario Argento's *Suspiria* is poetic, chaotic, and intriguing. Intoxicating visuals collide with its unrelenting prog-rock soundtrack to sweep the audience into the same frenzied sensory vortex as the film's protagonist, American ballet student Suzy Bannion. The cult reputation of Argento's baroque nightmare is reflected in the critical praise it continues to receive almost 40 years after its original release. For the majority of critics, *Suspiria* is not only the director's masterpiece, but also the zenith of Italian horror full stop: as Joe Bob Briggs put it, it is 'the *Gone With the Wind* of Eyetalian horror'.[1] As such, it regularly appears in lists of the best horror films of all time, and both *The Village Voice* and *Empire* magazine feature it in their lists of the greatest films ever made. For its many fans, *Suspiria* is synonymous with European horror more broadly, and Argento himself is by far the most famous of all the Italian horror directors. Kim Newman has observed, 'what Sergio Leone is to the Spaghetti Western, Dario Argento is to the Italian horror film'.[2] If there was any doubt of his status as one of the great horror auteurs, Argento's international reputation was solidified well beyond the realms of cult fandom in the 1990s with retrospectives at both the American Museum of the Moving Image and the British Film Institute.

For fans and critics alike, *Suspiria* is as mesmerising as it is impenetrable: the film itself even explicitly tells us its story is 'so absurd, so fantastic.' The film's bare commitment to aspects such as plot and characterisation combines with an aggressive stylistic hyperactivity, making *Suspiria* a film that needs to be experienced through the body as much as through the intellect. That *Suspiria* is so heavily loaded towards the senses, however, does not deny its fundamental artistry, but rather is integral to it. The absence of a complex storyline does not mean the one it has is anything less than wholly effective: the simplicity of its plot granted Argento the perfect loom upon which to weave his elaborate audio-visual tapestry. By refusing to privilege narrative and to reduce sound into the service of its visuals, *Suspiria* is simultaneously a rejection of the Classical Hollywood paradigm as much as it celebrates its Technicolor excesses and manic musicality.

This book considers the way that *Suspiria* entwines light, sound and cinema history to create one of the most breathtaking instances of the modern horror film. It is as fascinating as it is ultimately unfathomable. Argento's secret weapon is his invitation to not so much understand *Suspiria* intellectually as it is rather to experience it sensorially, and this holds the power to *Suspiria*'s ongoing allure. As the director noted in 2008, 'when you watch a movie, you understand your truth'.[3] It is in this spirit that this book does not seek to unlock any ultimate or singular hidden meaning within *Suspiria*, but rather it is a celebration of the myriad pleasures it offers. Unlike Suzy, we have no clandestine world to discover with the slow motion turn of a three-dimensional flower mural. After all, the secret of the irises was never really a secret at all: the supposed revelation that the ballet academy was run by a coven of witches was announced explicitly in the opening credits as the word "Witch!" hisses repeatedly throughout Goblin's haunting soundtrack. The mysteries of *Suspiria* lie in its kaleidoscope of experiences, influences, legacies, and histories, and it is these that this book will explore as it underscores its importance as one of the most daring, experimental and beautiful horror films ever made.

--

Witches have a long cinematic lineage, and while the fairy tale world of Walt Disney's *Snow White and the Seven Dwarfs* (1937)[4] might be the most overt influence on *Suspiria*, the iconography Argento was experimenting with has a long and diverse history in American film alone. Appearing in Classical Hollywood cinema most memorably in *The Wizard of Oz* (Victor Fleming, 1939), so omnipresent was the figure of the witch in the pop cultural imagination that it inspired a series of memorable romantic comedies, including René Clair's Veronica Lake-fronted *I Married a Witch* (1942), Richard Quine's 1958 film *Bell, Book and Candle* (starring post-*Vertigo* James Stewart and Kim Novak), culminating with the television series *Bewitched* in 1964. But witches had not been completely tamed, as demonstrated so memorably in movies such as Roger Corman's *The Undead* (1957), Argento's future collaborator George A. Romero's *Season of the Witch* (1973) and of course the blockbuster success of Roman Polanski's *Rosemary's Baby* (1968), a film that alone confirmed the place of witchcraft in twentieth-century horror.

Across Europe, movies about witchcraft have a long history, stretching at least back to the Swedish/Danish co-production *Häxan* (Benjamin Christensen, 1922). Although still difficult to acquire, *The Crucible* (*Les Sorcières de Salem*, Raymond Rouleau, 1957) was based on Arthur Miller's play written the year before, and was impressively adapted to the screen with a screenplay by noted French intellectual Jean-Paul Sartre. *Night of the Eagle* (Sidney Hayers, 1962) is a particularly memorable pre-*Suspiria* example of the subgenre, while in Germany, Michael Armstrong's *Mark of the Devil* (1970) was a successful attempt to profit on the earlier British Vincent Price film, *Witchfinder General* (Michael Reeves, 1968). In Italy, *Suspiria* was preceded by a number of significant films about witches including Mario Bava's *Black Sunday* (*La maschera del demonio*, 1960) and Corrado Farina's *Baba Yaga* (1973). The Dino De Laurentiis produced anthology *The Witches* (*Le streghe*, 1965) featured an impressive list of directors including Luchino Visconti, Pier Paolo Pasolini, and Vittorio De Sica, each of its five stories about witchcraft starring Silvana Mangano.

With *Suspiria*, Argento would aesthetically regenerate the cinematic witch. Inspired by the writings of Thomas De Quincey, the mythology established in the film would be expanded across Argento's two sequels, *Inferno* (1980) and *The Mother of Tears* (*La terza madre*, 2007). In one of *Suspiria*'s few moments of exposition, Dr Frank Mandel (Udo Kier) introduces the backstory of first mother, Helena Markos. He tells Suzy:

> Earlier in the Nineteenth Century, the Markos woman had been expelled from several European countries. She seemed to have something about her which urged religious people to persecute her. She also wrote a number of books, and I read that among the initiated, she went by the name The Black Queen. After she settled down here, she became the subject of a lot of gossip. Nevertheless, she managed to put her hands on a great deal of money, and she founded the Tanzakademie: at first a sort of school of dance and occult sciences. But that didn't last long, because in 1905, after being hounded and cursed at for ten years, Madame Markos died in a fire. That's all there is, as far as witchcraft is concerned. The school was taken over by her favourite pupil. The study of the occult was abandoned, and soon the place became the famous dance academy.

Mandel's colleague Professor Milius (Rudolf Schündler) elaborates further:

> (Witches) are malefic, negative and destructive. Their knowledge of the art of the
> occult gives them tremendous powers. They can change the course of events and
> people's lives, but only to do harm... Their goal is to accumulate great personal wealth,
> but that can only be achieved by injury to others. They can cause suffering, sickness
> and even the death... (Helena Markos) was a very famous black queen. A powerful
> witch with a tremendous talent for doing evil, a real mistress of magic. She lived and
> died in the city... A woman who becomes queen of her magic is a hundred times
> more powerful than the rest of the coven, which is like a serpent. Its strength rests
> with its leader: that is, with its head. A coven deprived of its leader is like a headless
> cobra: harmless.

Later in *Inferno*, a book called *The Three Mothers* written by alchemist and architect E.
Varelli is read by poet Rose (Irene Miracle) as the film begins. Through a voiceover, Varelli
says:

> I do not know what price I shall have to pay for breaking what we alchemists call
> Silentium. The life experience of our colleague should teach us not to upset laymen
> by imposing our knowledge upon them. I, Varelli, an architect living in London, met
> the Three Mothers and designed and built for them three dwelling places ... I failed
> to discover until too late that from these three locations the Three Mothers rule
> the world with sorrow, tears, and darkness ... And I built their horrible houses, the
> repositories of all their filthy secrets ... The land upon which the three houses have
> been constructed will eventually become deathly and plague-ridden, so much so that
> the area all around will reek horribly. And that is the first key to the mothers' secret,
> truly the primary key. The second key to the poisonous secret of the three sisters is
> hidden in the cellar under their houses. There you can find both the picture and the
> name of the sister living in that house. This is the location of the second key. The third
> key can be found under the soles of your shoes; there is the third key.

Although *Suspiria*'s story is often dismissed as one of its weakest elements, it provides
the foundations upon which the film's magical formal experimentation is built. Arriving in
Munich on a rainy night flight from New York, ballet student Suzy Bannion (Jessica
Harper) catches a taxi through the Black Forest to the esteemed Freiburg Tanzakedemie.

Inferno *(Dario Argento,*
1980)

At the door, she is refused entry and is told to come back tomorrow. After witnessing
an incident where another student leaves the dance school in a visibly distressed and
agitated state, the confused Suzy is forced to spend the evening elsewhere. The film
then turns its attentions to the upset student, Pat Hingle (Eva Axén), who has been
expelled from the academy and seeks the comfort of her friend Sonia (Susanna Javicoli),
who invites her to stay in her apartment for the evening. The distraught girl locks herself
in the bathroom to dry herself off after being stranded in the rainstorm. It is here that
the film's first act of violence occurs, when mysterious, disembodied eyes appear outside
the window looking in on the terrified Pat. Hairy arms smash through the window and
attack her graphically with a knife. As Sonia rushes to her assistance, she too meets a
similar fate: in the foyer of the building, Pat is hung from a large stained glass ceiling as
shards of falling metal and glass impale Sonia below.

Returning to the Tanzakademie the next morning, Suzy meets Madame Blanc (Joan
Bennett) and Miss Tanner (Alida Valli), who apologise for the previous evening's
confusion. Suzy is introduced to other students including Olga (Barbara Magnolfi),
whom Madame Blanc tells her will be her new housemate off campus rather than at the
Tanzakademie as originally planned. The next day, however, Madame Blanc has changed
her mind again and tells Suzy that she can now move back into the school as originally
planned. Suzy does not agree to this, but when she falls suddenly ill after a curious
encounter with one of the Tanzakademie's kitchen staff, she is forced to leave Olga's to
recover. Prescribed a daily glass of red wine by Professor Verdegast (Renato Scarpa), Suzy
develops a friendship with fellow student Sarah (Stefania Casini) who has a nearby room.

Before dinner, a shower of maggots falling from the ceiling traumatises the students, supposedly coming from a box of ruined food that was being stored in the building's attic. The Tanzakademie staff constructs makeshift accommodation in a large practice hall, with white sheets draped from the ceiling around the girls and their cot beds for privacy. During the evening, Sarah hears the sound of the mysterious Directress snoring, despite their being told she was away from the Tanzakademie. The sleeping figure of the Directress is revealed in silhouette behind the sleeping students.

Rehearsals the next morning are disrupted again when Miss Tanner confronts Daniel (Flavio Bucco), the blind piano player who provides the dancers' musical accompaniment. She accuses his seeing eye dog of biting the strange child Albert (Jacopo Mariani), Madam Blanc's nephew ('I'm very attached to him', Madam Blanc had told Suzy earlier). They argue bitterly in front of the pupils, with Daniel informing Miss Tanner that while he cannot see, his hearing is excellent and he is aware of what is going on at the Tanzakademie. Leaving a *bierhall* that evening and walking home through Munich's famous Königsplatz, bizarre shapes and sounds loom around Daniel. His obedient dog suddenly turns feral and attacks its owner, killing him in a scene drenched with blood.

Becoming increasingly curious about the peculiar goings-on at the dance school, Sarah tells the Suzy's that there is some confusion about where the staff go in the evenings. Listening carefully, she counts their footsteps. Despite insisting to Suzy that this is important, the American – drugged, it is implied, by the wine –is unable to focus on Sarah's desperate words. The next day, Suzy begins to recall what might be significant details about her brief encounter with Pat on the night of her arrival, recalling two words: 'iris' and 'secret'. Sarah tells Suzy while they are swimming that Pat had been behaving oddly for some time and had left written notes, but the girls discover these have vanished from Sarah's room. Again, Suzy finds herself unable to stay awake and therefore does not realise that Sarah is chased into the attic, where she too is killed.

Madame Blanc and Miss Tanner inform Suzy that Sarah has left the Tanzakademie without giving them any notice, an explanation Suzy does not believe. Contacting Sarah's friend Dr Frank Mandel (Udo Kier), the young psychologist tells Suzy the Tanzakademie's backstory. While Mandel is sceptical about black magic, his associate Professor Millus (Rudolf Schündler) is more open-minded, and tells Suzy that the coven's queen is vital to the survival of the group as a whole. Crucially, Suzy learns here that the only way to destroy the coven is to kill Markos herself.

Suzy returns to find the Tanzakademie empty, as the other students have left on a group excursion to the theatre. Recalling Sara's words about the sound of footsteps, Suzy counts them and traces them to Madame Blanc's office. Here she sees three-dimensional irises on a large wall mural, reminding her of Pat's until-then forgotten words before her death. Turning a blue flower, Suzy discovers a hidden corridor where she sees Madame Blanc, Miss Tanner and other Tanzakademie's staff engaged in a frightening ritual aimed at killing Suzy. Sneaking past them, she walks to the end of the corridor where she is menaced by Sarah's reanimated dead body, leading her to the terrifying figure of Helena Markos herself. When Markos supernaturally propels Sarah's corpse to attack Suzy, Suzy retaliates not by attacking her friend but by stabbing Markos' vague, disappearing-and-reappearing outline. Having dispatched the coven's queen, the building collapses around Suzy as she runs to safety in the street outside. Behind her, the Tanzakademie burns spectacularly as the film's end credits roll.

--

The image of Suzy blindly stabbing in the dark trying to locate the monstrous Helena Markos in *Suspiria*'s climax provides an apt metaphor for the experience of watching the film: like Suzy, success can only be achieved when logic gives way to intuition and we surrender to *feeling* our way through it rather than relying on common sense. In my own experience, this tendency is impossible to resist, no matter how hard one tries to approach the film from a more critical, objective position. There is something inherently out-of-reach about *Suspiria*, and it is this intangibility that has made it so enduring. Where we might normally find pleasure in complex characterisations or twisting plots, *Suspiria* urges us to discover new pleasures. The desire to articulate just what these may be is itself one of Argento central challenges. From this perspective, *Suspiria* is a film that invites us to surrender to the illogical, to be seduced by spectacle, and to revel in the pleasures of the senses. *Suspiria*'s sensory excesses are so overwhelming that they smother any intellectual strategies its audience may have to comprehend what is happening: as *The Village Voice*'s J. Hoberman noted in 2009, it is 'a movie that makes sense only to the eye'.[5]

With this emphasis on spectacle over narrative, *Suspiria* can usefully be approached through Tom Gunning's notion of the 'cinema of attractions', the ability of film to *show* something. This refers to 'an exhibitionist cinema … that displays its visibility, (and is) willing to rupture a self-enclosed fictional world for a chance to solicit the attention of the spectator'.[6] In early cinema, Gunning offers the example of actors looking directly into the camera to support this claim, but in the case of *Suspiria*, it can be powerfully demonstrated through its glut of overwhelming formal excesses. *Suspiria* continues the tradition of the cinema of attractions so vividly that it would at times be difficult to believe that it was purely accidental. When *Suspiria* is approached with this history in mind, it indicates a conscious attempt to acknowledge a legacy that narrative-heavy dominant cinema traditions have on the whole repressed. Every facet of *Suspiria* is laced with a knowing self-awareness that not only shuns but also aggressively mocks any attempt at realism.

Suspiria's cinematographer Luciano Tovoli tells a beautiful story about an early meeting with Argento that encapsulates how the film sought to privilege the senses. Tovoli's previous work as cinematographer was not particularly in keeping with the Gothic fairy tale Argento had had envisioned for the project, but despite Tovoli's doubts the director was certain he was the man for the job. Before committing, Tovoli asked Argento if he could run some technical tests to experiment with some of the ideas they had discussed. As Tovoli told noted Argento expert Alan Jones, 'Dario saw what I had done, went up and physically touched the screen and said it was fantastic'.[7]

The vision of Argento physically caressing the screen with Tovoli's early photographic experimentations emblazoned upon it is a powerful, hypnotic and deeply poetic image, one in tune with the film's intense haptic qualities. *Suspiria*'s audience does not need to touch the screen to feel it: in the spirit of Laura U. Marks' notion of haptic visuality,[8] its pleasures stem from the brush of its velvety, wet surfaces against our eyes (and, for that matter, our ears). Noël Carroll observed in his foundational book *The Philosophy of Horror, or Paradoxes of the Heart* (1990) that the very word 'horror' is rooted in an urgent and abnormal kind of physicality, stemming from both the Latin *horrere* and the old French word *orror*, both meaning to bristle or to shudder.[9] These origins highlight the centrality of corporeality to *Suspiria*, through sensations that every moment of the film seems so aggressively determined to remind us.

When discussing the films of Dario Argento, it is impossible to speak of bodies as a genderless whole, at least in terms of how he has been positioned in popular discourse. Before tackling the specifics of *Suspiria*, it necessary to address this perpetually sensitive issue from the outset. Argento has been plagued throughout his career with accusations of misogyny, particularly in relation to his representation of women as victims of graphic, glamorised and often highly sexualised murders. Negative estimations of Argento's gender politics have in large part been driven by what is with little doubt his most famous and commonly cited quotation, taken from an interview with Jones for *Cinefantastique* in 1983:

> I like women, especially beautiful ones…If they have a good face and figure, I would much prefer to watch them being murdered than an ugly girl or man. I certainly don't have to justify myself to anyone about this. I don't care what anybody thinks or reads into it. I have had journalists walk out of interviews when I say what I feel about this subject.[10]

When Carol J. Clover included the first half of this quote in her foundational book on feminist film theory, *Men, Women and Chainsaws: Gender in the Modern Horror Film* (1992), she offered it as seemingly clear cut evidence that some male horror film directors are unequivocally pigs. Becoming effectively canonised after its appearance in Clover's book, it is now virtually impossible to find any discussion about Argento and gender that doesn't refer to this quote or its sentiments as being inherent to the director's attitude towards women.

Which, to be fair, is understandable. In this longer version of the quote, Argento is unapologetic. But rather than taking a side in a binary debate on Argento's stance on gender and its representation in his films, it is possible to argue that the subject is far less black-and-white that this quote (and its privileging in broader debates on gender in horror) allows. In fact, many of Argento's films *deliberately* collapse the boundaries between 'male' and 'female' themselves: for instance, transsexual Eva Robins is the vamp in *Tenebre*'s pivotal primal scene, and in *Deep Red*, Carlo's gay lover is played by a woman. *Four Flies on Grey Velvet* tells of a female murderer who was raised as a boy, and so central was the indistinct gendering of the killer in *Cat O' Nine Tails* that they were even called the 'XXY killer'.

Argento's representations of gender, however, can at best be conceived as ambivalent. For instance, despite these examples of gender blurring, the problematic representation of homosexuality and lesbianism in *Mother of Tears*, *Tenebre* and *Four Flies on Grey Velvet* do not earn Argento awards for challenging stereotypes. These examples make it clear that trying to stake a claim for Argento as either completely progressive or regressive is ultimately futile: his work is too contradictory to allow it. This is perhaps nowhere more apparent than in his treatment of sexual violence. I have previously written at length about his rape-revenge film *The Stendhal Syndrome* (1996),[11] starring his daughter Asia as a policewoman investigating a series of sexual assaults who falls prey to the perpetrator she is tracking. Although the film has been often condemned for what some have assumed is its exploitative and sensational representation of rape, I have argued passionately that through its rigorous engagement with art historical and cinematic traditions, it strategically deconstructs the very representational mechanics through which rape has historically been depicted in the visual arts. It is a remarkable film, and still the director's most broadly misunderstood.

Again, however, *The Stendhal Syndrome* does not undo some of Argento's less tasteful engagements with sexual violence. In 1987, the series *The Nightmares of Dario Argento* (*Gli incubi di Dario Argento*) screened on Italian television network Radiotelevisione Italiana, and consisted of a series of short 3-minute episodes that Argento would himself introduce. 'To Love and Die' was a rape-revenge tale concerning a woman who was sexually assaulted by a masked man who broke into her house. Determined to seek revenge, she identifies three possible suspects in her neighbourhood, and the film follows as she seduces and has sex with each man until she identifies who raped her. It is during her sexual encounter with the last man that she realises he was responsible for her assault. She kills him with a large knife, squirming sexily as she is drenched in his blood.

While *The Stendhal Syndrome* ranks as one of the most sophisticated, self-aware and important rape-revenge films ever made, 'To Love and Die' falls firmly at the lower end of the scale. Its sensational, eroticized representation of sexual assault is offered for no other reason than to titillate and to appeal to the less-than-wholesome assumed perversities of its intended audience. Released nine years apart, the stark differences in the gender politics that manifest in *The Stendhal Syndrome* and 'To Love and Die' could simply mean that Argento learnt better. However, for some such as Donna de Ville and her scathing 2010 attack on *The Mother of Tears* (*La Terza Madre*, 2007), Argento's gender politics have hardly been solidly pro-women since *The Stendhal Syndrome*.

To pitch Argento's films against each other in an ideological death match is therefore futile. There are good arguments both for *and* against the director as progressive and regressive in relation to his depictions of gender. Taking this ambivalence into account, it therefore may be more fruitful to approach Argento and the eternally loaded gender issue from another perspective, one less concerned with how he sees women and one more interested with *how women see him*. As a starting point, it is worth emphasising that his films are certainly not lacking an appreciative female audience. In an interview on the 2010 Cine-Excess release of *Suspiria*, Argento said that he estimates approximately 60 per cent of his fan base are female. While he offers no concrete evidence for this, my own anecdotal experience does not consider this statistic at all inflated: most of the Argento fans I know are women, and his films are my first port of call when I am trying to woo an unconverted girlfriend to horror's broader delights.

For more empirical evidence that a love of Argento is not inherently opposed to progressive gender politics, however, one need only look to Kathy Acker. One of the most iconic feminists of the 1990s, Acker was an experimental author and proud Dario Argento fan, and crafted an explicit homage to the Italian horror director in her 1992 book, *My Mother: Demonology* (discussed further in Chapter Three). This is not a purely Western phenomenon. Renowned Japanese author Banana Yoshimoto has often cited Argento in interviews as an important influence. Also an admirer of Acker ('She was a real favourite of mine', she has said, 'I am sorry that she passed away before I had the chance to meet her'), Yoshimoto first saw *Suspiria* when she was 11-years-old:

I went to the cinema with my classmate and my older sister. It was the end of my dreamy Elementary school days and the beginning of my melancholy Junior high school life. My sister had just moved away to study so at the time everything seemed painful to me. His films deeply touched my heart. I found watching them a very healing process.

She wisely suggests that while Argento's influence might manifest most visibly in her and Acker's work, this does not mean they are the only two: 'I think many others have been influenced by his work, but perhaps not so blatantly'. Yoshimoto has described the personal impact of *Suspiria* beautifully, capturing what precisely it is about the film that leaves such a lasting impression on its many fans around the world: 'I learned from the movie that there is beauty even in solitude, that clearly malicious things can exist independently in the world, and that the presence of evil is possible'.[12]

Suspiria's lead actor Jessica Harper has provided a more immediate, first person reflection on Argento's relationship with women based on her experience working with him on the film. She spoke to Alan Jones highly of the Italian director:

> Dario didn't have a great command of the English language at the time so it wasn't always easy to communicate with him. But he had other abilities which led me to believe wholeheartedly that he was really smart and focused and absolutely sure about his aesthetic vision. I immediately found him to be interesting and compelling even though we had difficulty talking to each other. He was very supportive of what he thought my particular skills were.[13]

She also told Jones that she felt that Argento had rarely been given the credit he deserved for creating a vast number of interesting roles for women, which in *Suspiria* culminates in what was effectively an almost completely female ensemble cast. While there are a few small male roles in the film, Harper has rightly noted 'it was completely dominated by women'.[14] And unlike the sorority-centred slasher films that would explode in the genre during the late 1970s and 1980s – films that were inspired as much by Argento's earlier *gialli* films as they were Hitchcock's *Psycho* (1960) or Bob Clark's *Black Christmas* (1974) – *Suspiria* lacked the subgenre's otherwise omnipresent boob-shots. *Suspiria*'s strong women – Suzy herself, Miss Tanner and Madam Blanc – were built on robust personalities rather than cup size and age.

--

The following chapter will position *Suspiria* in the broader international horror cannon, considering it in the context of Argento's own *oeuvre*, and alongside other popular instances of the genre at the time. As the most critically acclaimed and beloved of all Italian horror directors, *Suspiria* marked a significant point in Argento's career as he turned from his earlier *gialli* (the 'Animal Trilogy' of *The Bird with the Crystal Plumage*

(*L'uccello dalle piume di cristallo*, 1970), *Four Flies on Grey Velvet* (*4 mosche di velluto grigio*, 1971) and *Cat O' Nine Tails* (*Il gatto a nove code*, 1971), and *Deep Red* (*Profondo Rosso* in 1975) to something more overtly supernatural. A number of factors intersected in the creation of the film, both collaboratively and in terms of Argento's own professional trajectory up to this point. One of the most fascinating aspects of *Suspiria* is the unique way it brought together a number of diverse influences, from Walt Disney's *Snow White and the Seven Dwarves* (1937) to Thomas de Quincey, whose laudanum-fuelled *Suspiria de Profundis* (1845) is referenced in the film's title. Argento's partner and *Deep Red* star Daria Nicolodi brought de Quincey's work to the directors attention, and along with a number of other key collaborators such as cinematographer Luciano Tovoli and rock band Goblin, *Suspiria* offers a useful place to consider the relationship between the director as auteur and their collaborators.

Chapter Two provides a scene-by-scene analysis of *Suspiria*, exploring the elements that hold it together as much as it celebrates the experimental spirit of that drove its bold, hallucinatory style. *Suspiria* is drenched with artfully deployed anarchy: consider, for instance, the fact that it is a film about a ballet school that features almost no dancing. It offers an explicit psychological explanation — as Dr Frank Mandel famously says, 'bad luck isn't brought by broken mirrors, but by broken minds' — and then does everything within its power to undermine such rationalisations. The most excessive aspects of *Suspiria* stem from its formal construction. Light, sound, colour, and movement converge with an intensity rendered all the more overpowering due to the film's perpetual fascination with the spectacle of suffering bodies. Less a singular narrative whole than an episodic string of viscera-rich vignettes, it is the mastery with which these scenes are constructed that has granted *Suspiria* its enduring reputation. This chapter unpacks the minutiae of these sequences, celebrating the joyful paradox of its simultaneous cohesion and incoherence.

The final chapter explores *Suspiria*'s reception both at the time of its release and the ways new audiences have come to embrace it over the past four decades. It also considers its status as the first part of Argento's recently completed *Three Mothers* trilogy, followed by *Inferno* and *Mother of Tears*. *Suspiria*'s tentacles have a long reach, and this book will conclude with a final assessment of *Suspiria*'s legacy and influence across the arts, exploring why it is still considered one of the most original, powerful and enigmatic horror films ever made.

CHAPTER ONE: MAGIC IS EVERYWHERE – A PRE-HISTORY OF *SUSPIRIA*

Horror was not at the forefront of early Italian cinema, with movies like *Frankenstein's Monster* (*Il Mostro di Frankenstein*, Eugenio Testa, 1920) and *Malombra* (Carmine Gallone, 1917) being rare highlights in the nation's output in the genre until the appearance of directors like Mario Bava and Riccardo Freda during the 1950s and 1960s. Horror films until then were oddities, with the notable exception of movies like Alessandro Blasetti's *Dr Jekyll and Mr Hyde*-inspired *The Haller Case* (*Il Caso Haller*) in 1933. But with films such as *Black Sabbath* (1963) and *Black Sunday* (*La maschera del demonio*, 1960), Mario Bava in particular became a key figure in the explosion of Italian horror that would mark the 1960s, 1970s and 1980s. While Bava's name may be the most immediately recognisable to non-Italian audiences, Riccardo Freda is historically just as important, if not more. Bava both co-directed and photographed two Freda films that are frequently considered the birthplace of Italian horror, *The Devil's Commandment* (*I vampiri*, 1957) and *Caltiki, The Immortal Monster* (*Caltiki, il mostro immortale*, 1959). Following in Bava and Freda's footsteps, 1960 saw a steady stream of Italian horror films, including Piero Regnoli's *The Playgirls and the Vampire* (*L'ultima preda del vampire*), Renato Polselli's *The Vampire and the Ballerina* (*L'amante del vampire*), Anton Giulio Majano's *Atom Age Vampire* (*Seddok, l'erede di Satana*) and Giorgio Ferroni's *Mill of the Stone Women* (*Il mulino delle donne di pietra*). Freda would continue to produce horror films such as 1962's *The Horrible Secret of Dr. Hichcock* (*L'orribile segreto del dottor Hichcock*) and *The Ghost* (*Lo sprettro*, 1963), alongside other key directors from this period like Antonio Margheriti (*The Castle of Terror* (*La danza macabre*) and the similarly English-titled *Horror Castle* (*La vergine di Norimberga*), both from 1963), and Massimo Pulillo, with films such as *Bloody Pit of Horror* (*Il boia scarlatto*, 1965), and *The Vengeance of Lady Morgan* (*La vendetta di Lady Morgan*) and *Terror Creatures from the Grave* (*Cinque tombe per un medium*), both in 1966.

There is a long history to Italy's cultural fascination with dark, viscera-intensive beauty. As has been recounted on numerous occasions – often by Argento himself – Italy's visual cultural history is one where beautiful violence has flourished. As James Gracey eloquently summarised, 'the great Italian Renaissance artists such as Michelangelo, Da Vinci and Caravaggio created baroque and majestic works of art celebrating the volatility of their heritage. The darkly romantic texts of Boccacio and Dante revel in hellish descriptions of live burials and descents into Hell'. He continues, 'Opera, too, is deeply passionate and contains violent outbursts and perverse love and death. The voyeuristic impulse to watch scenes of violence is thousands of years old'.[15]

While straightforward horror genre entries were comparatively thin on the ground in Italian cinema before the 1950s, the elements that would later overlap in a distinctly identifiable Italian horror were already in circulation, particularly in terms of sexuality and violence. For example, Italian silent era superstar Francesca Bertini was one of the first movie stars who showed her arms and breasts, and bloodshed was privileged in the sword-and-sandal films that were popular during the 1950s to the mid 1960s. As Gracey suggested, both *gialli* and the Spaghetti Westerns were united through their shared fascination with 'violence, sex and glorified death'.[16]

Translating simply to 'yellow' in English, the origins of *giallo* are in the yellow-covered mystery pulps that publishing house Mondadori began issuing during the 1920s. These were often translations of English-language stories by Edgar Wallace and Agatha Christie, and straddled horror and crime thriller genres. Cinematic *giallo* also had its own distinct iconography, most notably the ubiquitous black-gloved hands of the killer and an emphasis on graphic violence and sex. *Gialli* have an affinity for flamboyant, overly poetic titles like Argento's *The Bird with the Crystal Plumage* (*L'uccello dalle piume di cristallo*, 1970) and *Four Flies on Grey Velvet* (*4 mosche di velluto grigio*, 1971). Perhaps inspired by the success of Argento's early *gialli*, these kinds of titles became a *giallo* trademark, demonstrated in titles like *Five Dolls for an August Moon* (*5 bambole per la luna d'agosto* Mario Bava, 1970), *Short Night of Glass Dolls* (*La corta notte delle bambole di vetro*, Aldo Lado, 1971), *The House with Laughing Windows* (*La casa dalle finestre che ridono*, Pupi Avati, 1976), its elaborateness arguably peaking with *Your Vice Is a Locked Room and Only I Have the Key* (*Il tuo vizio è una stanza chiusa e solo io ne ho la chiave*, Sergio Martino, 1972) and *What Are Those Strange Drops of Blood on Jennifer's Body?* (*Perché quelle strane gocce di sangue sul corpo di Jennifer?*, Guiliano Carnimeo, 1971). *Giallo* has a distinct auteurist canon that includes both Mario Bava and his son Lamberto, Umberto Lenzi, Sergio Martino, Lucio Fulci, Luciano Ercoli, and Argento himself.

Bava's *The Girl Who Knew Too Much* (1963) and *Blood and Black Lace* (1964) are key movies in the early development of *gialli*, and he is widely held to be father of the category. Bava had by this time already achieved a high degree of success with Gothic horror films such as *The Whip and the Body* (1963), *Black Sabbath* and *Black Sunday*. The latter starred British actress Barbara Steele in one of her most iconic roles, and her famous pierced visage is still one of the most immediately recognisable images the Italian genre has produced. The roots of the kind of dark sexuality Steele personified in Italian horror during this period can be located within the early *Divismo* films and their unique version of the *femme fatale*.[17] While this *femme fatale* figure was visible in the historical dramas of the 1950s, through Steele Bava paid homage to this legacy in the context of the horror film. In turn, through his admiration of Bava, Argento's predilection for strong yet frequently morally ambivalent (or outright villainous) female characters is a further continuation of this strand of earlier Italian cinema.

The legacy of both Freda and Bava's work is imprinted across Dario Argento's *oeuvre* in a number of other ways. In the case of Freda, Argento himself has cited both *The Terror of Dr Hichock* (1962) and *The Ghost* (1963) as inspirations. Bava's influence manifests in *Suspiria* most overtly through the colour-drenched visual intensity that recalls *Kill Baby Kill* (1966), *Black Sabbath* and *The Whip and The Body*, along with the delight he takes in the execution of its numerous lavish, graphic murders. Argento has referred to both Mario Bava and Sergio Leone as his 'spiritual guides in the film world',[18] and he fell in love with the work of both directors during his time working as a film critic.

That Argento would begin his career as a movie critic makes sense. His father Salvatore Argento was a well-regarded film industry player. So vivid was young Dario's experience as a child growing up within the Italian film industry that he has often recalled that his earliest memory was sitting on Sophia Loren's knee. Like Martin Scorsese, Argento's poor health as a child led him to escape into the fictional worlds offered by books and movies, bestowing upon him an intense, informal training regime for his later career. Along with his mother Elda Luxardo and an uncle who were both successful photographers, the camera would be a defining presence in the young Argento's life. As he told Alan Jones, 'I was definitely born into the movies'.[19]

Argento initially had little desire to make movies, and was more interested in being a writer. With no interest in going to university, he falsified his age to secure a job as a film critic with the newspaper *Paese Sera*, whose minimum age limit requirement for its employees was 21. It was as a film critic that Argento would first meet Sergio Leone, whose impact on him would be great. He told Alan Jones of his meeting with Leone, 'it was the first time in my life that I had ever encountered a person who reasoned in terms of images. Every time he spoke, my brain would be flooded with some new, fantastical vision'.[20] Leone hired Argento and Bernardo Bertolucci to write *Once Upon a Time in the West* (*C'era una volta il West*, 1968), and between 1968 and 1970 Argento worked on a number of projects in a scriptwriter capacity, such as *Commandos* (Armando Crispino, 1968), *Battle of the Commandos* (*La Legione dei Dannati*, Umberto Lenzi, 1968), *Today We Kill, Tomorrow We Die!* (*Oggi a Me…Domani a Te*, Tonino Cervi, 1968) and *The Rope and the Colt* (*Cimitero Senza Croci*, Robert Hossein, 1968). He also co-wrote the script for *One Night at Dinner* (*Metti, Una Sera a Cena*, Giuseppe Patroni Griffi, 1969), starring Jean-Louis Trintignant that would be entered in the 1969 Cannes Film Festival. The other major cinematic influences Argento has identified are perhaps unsurprising for a director with a background as an European film critic. He has cited Alfred Hitchcock, Michelangelo Antonioni, Jean Luc Godard, Luis Buñuel, Alain Resnais, Ingmar Bergman, Jacques Tourneur, Carl Theodor Dreyer, Fritz Lang and F.W. Murnau, all of whom have left marks both overt and subtle on Argento's own movies since he first began directing in 1970.

With its very name taken from Thomas de Quincey's *Suspiria De Profundis*, Argento's film also wears its literary heritage on its sleeve. Co-writer Daria Nicolodi has listed *Snow White*, *Bluebeard* and *Alice in Wonderland* as influences upon her work on *Suspiria*, and Argento has said that children's literature more broadly left a strong mark on how he worked his way through the witchcraft elements so central to the movie. Of all the creative works that left the strongest impression on him and his work, however, Argento has frequently cited Edgar Allan Poe as perhaps the most influential. The American author's obsessions with sex, death, violence and memory manifest across Argento's films in diverse ways in the creation of his own nightmare universes.

The visual arts have also made a deep impression on Argento's films. Both Austrian Expressionist Oskar Kokoschka and Dutch graphic artist M. C. Escher are mentioned explicitly in *Suspiria*'s script, and Argento's films are often described as having painterly qualities. This is certainly the case with *Inferno*, and also obviously applies to *Suspiria*. It is perhaps this aspect of Argento's work that has positioned him as a central art-horror auteur, aligning his movies alongside other key entries in this category such as *Eyes Without a Face* (*Les yeux sans visage*, Georges Franju, 1960), *Carnival of Souls* (Herk Harvey, 1962), *Repulsion* (Roman Polanski, 1965) and *Hour of the Wolf* (Vargtimmen, Ingmar Bergman, 1968).

Significantly, however, the role of the visual arts in Argento's films functions far more explicitly than this art-horror context would suggest. Whether it is the deployment of paintings by great masters such as Bruegel, Botticelli and Carravagio in *The Stendhal Syndrome* (*La sindrome di Stendhal*, 1996), the killer sculpture in *Tenebre* (1982), or the paintings that prove central to unravelling the mysteries of *Suspiria* and *Deep Red*, Argento's plots are regularly built around works of art across his oeuvre. This is nowhere more vivid than in Argento's first film as director, the *giallo The Bird with the Crystal Plumage* (*L'uccello dalle piume di cristallo*, 1970). Aside from the inclusion of a vital, clue-bearing painting and a killer sculpture, like *The Stendhal Syndrome* the events that launch their protagonist's journeys both take place in an art gallery.

The Bird with the Crystal Plumage *(Dario Argento, 1970)*

Tiring of his work as a gun-for-hire, Argento became a director out of necessity rather than anything else, as it was simply the most logical way he could see his scripts best brought to the screen. His work on the script for *One Night at Dinner* (*Metti, una sera a cena*, Giuseppe Patroni Griffi, 1969) consolidated his relationship with two individuals who would prove crucial to *The Bird with the Crystal Plumage*, actor Tony Musante (who would play Argento's protagonist, Sam Dalmas), and producer Goffredo Lombardo. According to Louis Paul, Bernardo Bertolucci introduced Argento to Frederic Brown's 1949 pulp novel *The Screaming Mimi*, upon which *The Bird with the Crystal Plumage* is unofficially based. When Bertolucci's attempt to adapt the book did not transpire, Argento – inspired by Bava's *The Girl Who Knew Too Much* (*La Ragazza Che Sapeva Troppo*, 1962), with which it shares a number of stylistic and narrative elements – wrote the script and started production. Although co-producer Lombardo was initially displeased with Argento's performance as director and even attempted to replace him with Ferdinando Baldi, Argento persevered and his debut film proved a commercial and critical success. It grossed approximately 1,650,000,000 Italian Lira domestically, almost double its production costs. It was nominated for an Edgar Allan Poe award in 1971 for best film, and of the movie Argento has said, 'it was a great first experience'.[21]

On the back of *The Bird with the Crystal Plumage*'s success, Argento had no trouble financing his next film, *The Cat O' Nine Tails* (1971). But the project – one of Argento's least favourite of his films – was a double-edged sword as the pressure to relive the glory of his previous film restricted the opportunity for creative autonomy. Starring Karl Malden as the film's blind investigator Franco and assisted by his young niece Lori (Cinzia De Carolis), according to long-time collaborator Luigi Cozzi the film's influences include Robert Sidomak's film noir *The Spiral Staircase* (1946) and Roy Boulting's 1968 movie *Twisted Nerve*[22] (known primarily today for its Bernard Hermann musical motif, made famous in 2003 by Quentin Tarantino's *Kill Bill*). A hit in Italy and across Europe, it failed to equal the success of its predecessor in the United States due in part to the lacklustre performance of distributor National-General Pictures. But contemporary fans and critics have recently reappraised *The Cat O' Nine Tails*, many determined to grant it the title of one of the director's most unfairly underrated works.

Four Flies on Grey Velvet (1971) was for many years the Holy Grail for Eurohorror fans due to the near-impossibility of finding a copy, legitimately or otherwise. An official DVD release in 2009 afforded many Argento devotees a long-awaited conclusion to the Animal Trilogy in one of his most visually interesting movies, forming a clear stylistic and thematic bridge to *Deep Red* in particular with its visuals and heavy-handed Oedipal themes. The film follows Roberto Tobias (Michael Brandon), a drummer who falsely believes he has killed a man. The film co-stars Mimsy Farmer as Tobias' wife in one of her most beautifully skittish Italian genre film performances and featuring a light-hearted cameo by Carlo 'Bud Spencer' Pedersoli as Godfrey (God for short). After the poor US distribution of *The Cat O' Nine Tails*, Paramount Pictures was charged with the global distribution of the third and final part of the *giallo* trilogy. This brought with it numerous demands, especially regarding the casting of Tobias: everyone from Terrance Stamp, Michael York, Jean-Louis Tringtignant, and even John Lennon and Ringo Starr were presented as potential options. Holding the rights to the film, Paramount were also primarily responsible for the film's scarcity.

At the completion of the *giallo* trilogy, Argento and his father Salvatore established the film production company SEDA Spettacoli to produce not only Dario's movies, but those by other directors. With long-time associate Luigi Cozzi, in 1972 Argento began work on an adaption of Mary Shelley's *Frankenstein* (1818) that failed to get off the ground, despite a young Timothy Dalton attached to it, fresh off the back of his performance in a series of historical dramas including the 1970 AIP production of *Wuthering Heights* by Robert 'Dr Phibes' Fuest, and smaller roles in the Oscar nominated *Mary, Queen of Scots* (Charles Jarrott, 1971) and *Cromwell* (Ken Hughes, 1970). Argento has suggested the project collapsed due the fact that Hammer and Universal (with whom he was hoping to develop the project) were uncomfortable restaging Shelley's classic horror story in the context of the Third Reich. To Argento and Cozzi's credit, they may have been ahead of their time if Richard Raaphorst's 2013 film *Frankenstein's Army* is anything to go by. Turning their attention to the smaller screen, Cozzi and Argento instead joined forces on the RAI four-part television series *Door into Darkness* in 1973.

Argento's next feature was the commercially and critically disastrous *The Five Days* (*Le Cinque Gionrnate*, 1973), an adventure/comedy/drama film with political undertones set during the Risorgimento period. Licking his wounds, despite previously wanting to step away from *gialli*, it seemed logical to return to the category that had brought him earlier acclaim. Thus was born one of his most famous and beloved films, *Deep Red* (*Profondo Rosso*, 1975). Filmed in Turin in 1974, it was important in Argento's career for a number of reasons, not least of which being that it was his first collaboration with Daria Nicolodi, who would have a tremendous effect on Argento both personally and professionally. It would also be the first time Argento worked with Goblin, and his collaborations with both the band and Nicolodi would flourish when renuinted on *Suspiria*. Joyful and macabre in equal measure, David Hemmings' protagonist Marc Daly bumbles through Argento's baroque mystery *Deep Red*, drenched in intelligence and energy as much as its eponymous deep red gore.

TOWARDS *SUSPIRIA*

With the success of *Deep Red* in Italy validating his intuitive flair for formal experimentation in the context of a commercial film genre, for his next project Argento now wanted to stretch the limits of horror even further. As he famously told Alan Jones, with *Deep Red*'s follow-up he wanted to take a 'quantum leap into the unknown'.[23] Argento had a long-held fascination with the occult, but critics are still divided about the relationship between *Suspiria*'s supernatural elements and the equally gruesome but decidedly of-this-world *giallo*. For some, the two can be neatly separated,[24] while for others they overlap.[25] Argento himself considers the question ultimately neither here nor there: as Maitland McDonagh noted in her foundational book on the director *Broken Mirrors/Broken Minds: The Dark Dreams of Dario Argento* (1991/1994/2010), 'I think that's an artificial distinction; I don't see a great difference between them. The realistic pictures are not very realistic, even though they're about psychopaths rather than witches'.[26]

Although he had previously toyed with an adaptation of Gaston Leroux's *Phantom of the Opera* (a project he would return to in 1998 in a movie version starring his daughter, Asia), the works of H.P. Lovecraft were initially more tempting. The idea of an Argento adaptation of Lovecraft's work is for many fans dizzying and tantalizing, with both horror icons sharing a talent for crafting vivid, hypersensory tales of terror. Ultimately, however, Argento felt that Lovecraft's vision may have restrained his own creativity, and that Lovecraft's stories were so complex and abstract that they would be difficult to do justice. Certainly the mediocre Lovecraft adaptations that have been produced indicate this may have been a wise move, although there are some exceptional examples like *Banshee Chapter* (Blair Erickson, 2013), *In the Mouth of Madness* (John Carpenter, 1995), *The Color Out of Space* (*Die Farbe*, Huan Vu, 2010), Stuart Gordon's *Re-Animator* (1985), and *Il mistero di Lovecraft – Road to L.* (Federico Greco and Roberto Leggio, 2005). The latter in particular is a useful indicator of how Lovecraft's horror universe can be moved to an Italian context, although it is likely Argento would have brought his own distinctive visual style to such a project well beyond the consciously amateur aesthetics of found footage horror.

At the root of his desire to make a film built around a supernatural premise was Argento's passion for Edgar Allan Poe, who he had cherished since childhood. Framed by this regression to the literary landscape of his youth, Argento became increasingly focused upon a folkloric figure that had haunted his young mind: witches. According to Argento, his interest in witchcraft was solidified the deeper he investigated it, traveling across Europe to meet many women who practiced the black arts. During this research period, he discovered one book in particular that talked about a girl's school where magical skills were taught to its students. In an interview with Stephen Daultrey in 2009, Argento flatly rejected claims by his co-writer Daria Nicolodi that the film was based on stories she shared with Argento about her grandmother's experience as a teen in a music school near the Swiss town of Basle that was a front for a coven ('that story was made up', said Argento).[27] Whether fictional or not, however, Nicolodi's input into the creation of *Suspiria*'s script is undeniable, as is the allure of the stories she has told about her remarkable grandmother, an ex-lover of Jean Cocteau and a practicing white witch, whose healing powers Nicolodi herself believes to have inherited.

While the issue of who-brought-what to the *Suspiria* project was clearly a bone of contention for some time, there is little doubt that it was the spark between Argento and Nicolodi – both professionally and personally – that was in large part where *Suspiria* attained its palpable energy. As one of the great off-screen love stories of European cinema, their relationship and its collapse was a magnet for media attention in Italy, with Alan Jones comparing it at one stage to the press frenzy that surrounded Elizabeth Taylor and Richard Burton.[28] In an interview with Jones, Dario's brother Claudio described this relationship: 'They lived together, loved each other, hated each other and screamed at each other – endlessly … from the artistic point of view their union was very positive on the creative front. From the domestic point of view it was a nightmare'.[29]

Nicolodi's status as one of the most important women in Eurohorror refers to her work both behind and in front of the camera. Her screen presence is one of Italian horror cinemas most enduring and hypnotic, even for audiences today. While her film work is associated most immediately with Argento, she has appeared in movies directed by horror luminaries including Michele Soavi, and both Mario Bava and his son Lamberto. In 2000, she appeared in her and Dario's daughter Asia's directorial debut, the semi-autobiographical *Scarlet Diva*, and also played Asia's mother in the final instalment of the Three Mothers trilogy, *The Mother of Tears* (*La Terza Madre*, 2007). Off camera, her work has been just as important. Nicolodi travelled with Argento as they researched real-life witchcraft while working on the original script for *Suspiria*, and in these earlier stages of the film's preparation she was even pegged to appear as Suzy's friend Sarah: it was only after Nicolodi dislocated her ankle during a rehearsal that her role was reduced to a brief cameo in the airport at the beginning of the film.[30]

Asia Argento holds a photograph of Daria Nicolodi in The Mother of Tears *(Dario Argento, 2007)*

Perhaps most crucially, it was Nicolodi who read Thomas De Quincey and identified within his story of the Three Mothers the foundations for a horror film. Named after the first mother – the Mother of Sighs – Nicolodi shrewdly recognised in 'Suspiria' the perfect name for the type of horror film Argento was wanting to make. Thomas De Quincey's name is synonymous with the feverish, drug-induced romanticism that marked his most popular work, *Confessions of an English Opium Eater*.[31] Detailing the wild hallucinations that his laudanum habit afforded him, the book brought De Quincey rapid success, aligning him with friends Samuel Coleridge and Williams Wordsworth as one the nineteenth century's most memorable English writers. Less the literal documentation of his drug-induced visions than an experiment in using those visions as the basis for his vivid style of writing, his following book *Suspiria De Profundis* (*Sighs from the Depths*) sat somewhere between poetry and prose. Of these essays, it is 'Levana and Our Ladies of Sorrow' that De Quincey introduced Mater Suspiriorum (Our Lady of Sighs), Mater Lachrymarum (Our Lady of Tears), and Mater Tenebrarum, Our Lady of Darkness, three companions for Levana, the Roman goddess of childbirth.

An analysis of the relationship between De Quincey's work and Argento's film should naturally drift towards the former's provision of the basic mythology that structures the horror trilogy, combined with the hallucinatory intensity of both *Suspiria* and *Inferno*'s audio-visual qualities in particular. But in her essay 'Living a Ruined Life: De Quincey Beyond the Worst' (2009), Rei Terada notes that De Quincey's *Suspiria de Profundis* is a meditation on the trauma he suffered with the death of his sister Elizabeth. It is from this perspective, Terada suggests, that De Quincey's work 'accounts for what happens when the mind does understand what no one should be able to understand'.[32] Taken in the context of Argento's film, this observation opens up fresh new ways to consider the relationship between De Quincey and Argento as Suzy grapples with how to conceive the inconceivable: that she has enrolled in a ballet school run by a coven of murderous witches. Via Terada, the assumption that Suzy has been dropped into an abnormal, physically overwhelming world can be conceived differently: the incomprehensible events surrounding Suzy can *only make sense* in a world this weird. From this more subjective viewpoint, Suzy's perception can be argued to be adapting to the strangeness of her new environment.

This hyperactive domain of the young imagination aligns *Suspiria* with a literary heritage just as important to the film as De Quincey's – that of the fairy tale. In his foundational work *The Philosophy of Horror: Or, Paradoxes of the Heart* (1990), Noël Carroll identifies the thin line that separates horror stories from fairy tales. While in the former monsters are considered something unusual, in the latter they are part of everyday life. In horror 'the monster is an extraordinary character in our ordinary world, whereas in fairy tales and the like the monster is an ordinary creature in an extraordinary world'.[33] From this perspective, it makes sense to talk about *Suspiria* as a fairy tale. The lurid, hallucinatory diegetic Argento created is one where the presence of witches makes complete sense. He also brings to life the bodily violence that permeated the stories of the Brothers Grimm. One of the reasons for the film's enduring appeal is precisely because it so intensely recalls a logic we learn as children: the dark, demented and alluring sensibility of the fairy tale. Asia Argento saw *Suspiria* for the first time when she was about six-years-old. 'I loved it', she said in an interview in 2007. 'It was like a fairy tale; a mean fairy tale. For me, I wasn't so shocked by it because I really saw it like Hansel and Gretel. It was just like all these really mean fairy tales that I loved as a child'.[34]

In 2001, Adrian Horrocks' presented one of the most intriguing readings of *Suspiria*'s relationship to these fairy tale qualities. Drawing a parallel between Dorothy's journey's beyond Depression-riddled Kansas of the interwar period and Suzy's arrival in Germany from America, Horrocks presents a compelling case for *Suspiria* to be understood as a dark retelling of the 1939 MGM screen adaptation of L. Frank Baum's *The Wonderful Wizard of Oz* (1900). Like *Suspiria*, it follows an innocent girl who travels through a portal into a vivid, Technicolor fantasy space, marked by a glut of colour and music. Dorothy's voyage of self-discovery manifests in *Suspiria* as Suzy's journey towards understanding and conquering the dark forces of the adult world, the yellow brick road replaced by the Tanzakademie's seemingly endless labyrinthine corridors.

But if there is one fairy tale consistently discussed in relation to *Suspiria*, it is *Snow White*; particularly Walt Disney's 1937 animated production of which Argento has stated on numerous occasions was a direct inspiration on his film's colour palette. Desiring the cartoon-like intensity of Disney's adaptation, Argento's construction of *Suspiria* as a twisted fairy tale stems well beyond the film's cinematography. After seeing a group of young children performing ballet in Germany, Argento originally wanted the movie to focus on much younger girls (aged from 10 to 14 years old, according to different accounts). He was encouraged to use an older cast, based on concerns that including children may result in the film either getting banned or being unable to get funding from financiers (an early draft of the film was about children being tortured by their teachers). To maintain this sense of scale – of small children in a big, scary world – *Suspiria* was strategically designed to maintain this feeling. Most famously, this included placing door handles very high up so that its actors would have to reach upwards, just like young children. Where *Suspiria* deviates from Disney's *Snow White* is in its story's ultimate purpose: while the animated classic speaks of a world where love conquers all, Argento's narrative universe is one where logic and reason are destabilized and subverted.

SUSPIRIA'S CAST

Suspiria was shot on location in Munich and West Barvaria in 1976, followed by interior shooting in Argento's reconstructed dance school at Rome's De Paolis Studios. Argento has recalled that his time filming *Suspiria* in Munich was shrouded by a suitably dark mystique, with his arrival marked by churches being surrounded by black flags as the city mourned one of its Archbishops. He also remembers it being a pleasant shoot, with most days concluding with the drinking of beer, joined at times by luminaries such as Rainer Werner Fassbinder and David Bowie.

Amongst its strengths, *Suspiria* is a shrewdly cast women's ensemble film led by a number of strong performers. So striking is the presence of actors like Jessica Harper, Alida Valli and Joan Bennett that even to those of us familiar with the film it takes some effort to recall where, when and why the film's few male characters appear. Born in 1949, *Suspiria*'s star Jessica Harper may have turned 28 in the year that the film was released, but she brought what Stephen Thompson has perfectly described as 'an unsurpassed 40-year-old-woman-in-the-body-of-a-14-year-old-girl oddness'[35] to the role of Suzy Banyon. Before *Suspiria*, the Chicago-born Harper's major performances were characters that straddled innocence and experience. The first of these was as Cathy Cake in John Byrum's debut feature *Inserts* in 1974. Appearing alongside Richard Dreyfuss, Bob Hoskins and Veronica Cartwright, Harper's Cathy is an aspiring porn actress in this adult tale of the underbelly of 1930s Hollywood.

Making a short but memorable appearance in Woody Allen's *Love and Death* in 1975 (she would later appear in his 1980 movie *Stardust Memories*), Harper came to Argento's attention through her role as Phoenix in Brian De Palma's glorious musical *Phantom of the Paradise* (1974), which was a huge hit in Italy despite initially bombing in the United States. A glittery rock operatic retelling of the *Phantom of the Opera* through a Faustian lens, Harper's Phoenix is an aspiring singer whose success is marked by the rise and fall of the film's male protagonist Winslow Leach (William Finney) and the villainous Swan (Paul Winslow). Harper liked Argento's earlier films and was attracted by the creative opportunities that working with the Italian director might bring. Combined with the idea of working and living in Rome, she accepted the role of Suzy. Although she had trained as a dancer, this was of little interest to Argento.

With her pale face framed by dark hair and bold eyebrows, as Stanley Manders has observed *Suspiria*-era Harper struck a remarkable similarity to Disney's Snow White.[36] Her looks were also reminiscent of a Classical Hollywood brunettes like Elizabeth Taylor,

(top) Jessica Harper in Phantom of the Paradise (Brian De Palma, 1974); (centre) Joan Bennett in Scarlet Street (Fritz Lang, 1945); (bottom) Alida Valli in The Paradine Case (Alfred Hitchcock, 1947)

Hedy Lamar, Deanna Durbin, and significantly, a young Joan Bennett, the latter of whom would appear alongside her in *Suspiria* as Madam Blanc. Harper had confided in an interview with Alan Jones that at the time of filming she was concerned that Bennett's background as a Classical Hollywood star may have brought a *prima donna* aspect to the set, but was pleasantly surprised by Bennett's kindness despite her shaky health.

Like Argento, Bennett was born into show business. Her grandfather, grandmother, parents and two sisters were all actors, and she first appeared on screen in the silent film *The Valley of Decisions* (1916) when she was only six years old. With a successful career spanning early cinema, classical Hollywood and television, her performance as the *femme fatale* in Fritz Lang's *The Woman in the Window* (1944) and *Scarlet Street* (1945) no doubt left an impression on Argento. By the 1970s, she was a familiar face to television audiences due to her starring role in the gothic soap *Dark Shadows* from 1966 to 1971 (a series recently celebrated in Tim Burton's 2012 film of the same name) and its film spin-off, *The House of Dark Shadows* (Dan Curtis, 1970). *Suspiria* does not dwell on the similarity of Harper to the younger Bennett, although this certainly adds to the thematic maternal undercurrents that run throughout. Bennett's evocation of the monstrous feminine is playfully evoked by James Gracey's observation that Madam Blanc physically recalls Bette Davis' character in *Whatever Happened to Baby Jane?* (Robert Aldrich, 1962). However the greatest description of Bennett's Blanc still goes to Alan Brien, who compared her to 'a waxwork Princess Margaret'.[37]

As one of the great stars of Italian cinema, Alida Valli's performance as Miss Tanner sits alongside many career highlights on stage and screen including Alfred Hitchcock's *The Paradine Case* (1947), Michelangelo Antonioni's *The Cry* (*Il Grido*, 1957) Luchino Visconti's *Senso* (1954), Bernardo Bertolucci's *Novecento* (1900, 1976), *Luna* (*La Luna*, 1979), and *The Spider's Stratagem* (*La strategia del ragno*, 1970), Pier Paolo Pasolini's *Oedipus Rex* (*Edipo Re*, 1967), and Carol Reed's *The Third Man* alongside Orson Welles and Joseph Cotten. For fans of Eurohorror, Valli was recognisable from films like Mario Bava's *Lisa and the Devil* (*Lisa e il diavolo*, 1974) *Confessions of a Blood Drinker* (*Tendre Dracula*, Pierre Grunstein, 1974), *The Antichrist* (*L'anticristo*, Alberto De Martino, 1974) and of course Georges Franju's art-horror classic, the beautiful 1960 bio-shocker *Eyes Without a Face* (*Les yeux sans visage*). Across her long career, Valli performed convincingly in an array of different characters, but those that are the most memorable today – of which *Suspiria*'s

Miss Tanner is certainly at the forefront – are those that most powerfully brought to life a distinctive kind of strength, whether it be Hitchcock's *femme fatale* Maddalena Anna Paradine, or as Mother Superior in Giulio Berruti's exquisite nunsploitation hot mess, *Killer Nun* (*Suor Omicidi*, 1978).

Suzy's friend Sarah was played by Stefania Casini, who before *Suspiria* had attained small roles in Dennis Berry's *The Big Delirium* (*Le Grand Délire*, 1975), Paul Morrissey's 1974 film *Blood for Dracula* (with *Suspiria* co-star Udo Kier), and Bernado Bertolucci's *1900* (*Novocento*, 1976), with another *Suspiria* co-star, Alida Valli. After *Suspiria*, Casini would appear in classic art films such as Peter Greenaway's *The Belly of an Architect* (1987) and *Andy Warhol's Bad* (Jed Johnson, 1977), as well as Antonio Bido's *giallo The Bloodstained Shadow* (*Solamente nero*) in 1978. Swedish actor Eva Axén played the ill-fated Pat Hingle, an actor who was discovered by Luchino Visconti and appeared in a small, uncredited role in his celebrated 1971 film, *Death in Venice*. Smaller roles were Barbara Magnolfi as the snippy, sexy dance student Olga, who had earlier appeared in Sergio Martino's *The Suspicious Death of a Minor* (1975) and would later star in Enzo Milloni's nasty *giallo Sister of Ursula* (1978). And while a minor character, Franca Scagnetti's performance as the cook who flashes the light into Suzy's eyes is for many of *Suspiria*'s fans (myself included) the film's most captivating character. Scagnetti was a familiar face in Italian cinema and was in over 80 films during her 30 year career. Coincidentally, her two roles before *Suspiria* – *Donna... cosa si fa per te* (Giuliano Biagetti, 1976) and *Cuginetta... amore mio!* (Bruno Mattei, 1976) – saw her again cast as housekeeping staff.

Although only a minor character in the film, German actor Rudolf Schündler's role as Professor Milius was a coup for *Suspiria*. As Chris and Regan McNeil's domestic Karl in William Friedkin's horror blockbuster *The Exorcist* in 1973, Schündler – who had by this stage a lengthy career on the screen, with highlights including Fritz Lang's *The Testament of Dr. Mabuse* (*Das Testament des Dr. Mabuse*, 1933) – if not a readily known name internationally, was certainly at least a very familiar face. Similarly, there is little denying the cult status of German actor Udo Kier, and alongside early performances in *The Story of O* (Just Jaeckin, 1975), and Paul Morrissey's *Flesh for Frankenstein* (1973) and *Blood for Dracula* (1974), his role in *Suspiria* in large part provided the foundations for his cult reputation. Kier has recounted to Alan Jones that he was filming with Rainer Werner Fassbinder in Munich when he first heard from Argento about the role of Dr. Frank

Rudolf Schündler in The Exorcist *(William Friedkin, 1973)*

Mandel. According to Kier, Argento was insistent that Kier was the only person who could successfully deliver the film's infamous 'bad luck isn't brought by broken mirrors, but by broken minds' speech. Despite understanding little of the script because of his then-limited English, he recalled Fassbinder was unhappy with his accepting the role: 'We were living together at the time and he got jealous for some reason but I was happy to play a small part in what turned out to be a horror classic'.[38]

Jacopo Mariani in Deep Red *(Dario Argento, 1975)*

There are a number of other male performers in *Suspiria* who are worthy of note. These include Flavio Bucci, who played blind piano player Daniel. Italian horror fans will recognise Bucci from his earlier chilling performance in Aldo Lado's *Night Train Murders* (*L'ultimo treno della notte*, 1975) alongside *Deep Red*'s Macha Merril, and in 1973 he appeared in Elio Petri's *Property is No Longer a Theft* (1973) with Daria Nicolodi. *Deep Red* also included a memorable appearance by Jacopo Mariani as the young Carlo, who looks almost identical in *Suspiria* as Albert, Madam Blanc's nephew. The young Mariani had previously appeared in a small capacity in the Ingrid Thulin-fronted war film *The Voyage Into the Whirlpool Has Begun* (*E cominciò il viaggio nella vertigine*, Toni de Gregorio, 1974), along with Renato Scarpa. As Professor Verdegast in *Suspiria*, Scarpa's performance was a welcome return to the screen for admirers of Nicolas Roeg's *Don't Look Now* (1973), where he played Inspector Longhin. Set in Venice, Roeg's breathtaking supernatural thriller was arguably inspired as much by Aldo Lado's *giallo Who Saw Her Die* (*Chi l'ha vista morire?*, 1972) as it was the 1971 short story by Daphne Du Maurier upon which it was based. Dance student Mark was played by Miguel Bosé, a Latin American musician with close family ties to the Italian film industry (his godfather was Luchino Visconti). Handyman Pavlo was played by Giuseppe Transocchi, who came to the part with good Italian horror form in the shape of an earlier appearance in Paolo Heusch's classic *Werewolf in a Girls' Dormitory* (1961), written by key *giallo* writer and director Ernesto Gastaldi. Finally, the taxi driver was played by Fulvio Mingozzi. While he famously appears driving another cab in *Inferno*, Mingozzi regularly appeared in Argento's films and can spotted in films from *The Bird with the Crystal Plumage* to *Phenomena*, as well as making brief appearances in classic Italian horror films like Freda's *Tragic Ceremony* (*Estratto dagli archivi segreti della polizia di una capitale europea*, 1972), Umberto Lenzi's *Seven Blood-Stained Orchids* (*Sette orchidee macchiate di rosso*, 1972), Paolo Cavara's *Black Belly of the Tarantula* (1971), and Sergio Martino's *The Case of the Scorpion's Tail* (*La coda dello scorpione*, 1971).

SUSPIRIA'S CREW

When it came to the crew for *Suspiria*, Argento turned in large part to filmmaking professionals who were already or would become part of his core filmmaking team. What Alan Brein described in 1977 as *Suspiria*'s 'elaborate, bilious, art-deco sets'[39] were the work of Production Designer Giuseppe Bassan, who had worked on *The Five Days* and *Deep Red* with Argento previously, and would continue this collaboration in *Tenebre* and as Art Director for *Inferno*. Beyond his work with Argento, Bassan was Set Decorator for Umberto Lenzi's cult favourite *Kriminal* (1966) and its sequel, *Il March di Kriminal* (Fernando Cerchio, 1968) as well as Massimo Dallamano's stylish *giallo A Black Veil for Lisa* (*La morte non ha sesso*, 1968). *Suspiria*'s costume designer Pierangelo Cicoletti would later also work on *Tenebre*, while Assistant Director Antonio Gabrielle would soon be First Assistant Director on *Opera*. *Suspiria*'s special effects were the result of Germano Natali's input, whose skills in this capacity had already been brought to the fore in *Deep Red*. Natali's talents were later put to use in *Inferno* and *Opera*, and in other beloved Italian horror classics such as Lucio Fulci's *The Beyond* (*L'aldilà*, 1981).

Suspiria's editor Franco Fraticelli began his very long career in the film industry with *È arrivato il cavaliere!* (Mario Monicelli and Steno, 1950). Fraticelli's career highlights include many films with Dario Argento, not just those Argento directed (*The Bird with the Crystal Plumage, Cat O' Nine Tails, Four Flies on Grey Velvet, The Five Days, Deep Red, Suspiria, Inferno, Tenebrea, Phenomena*, and *Opera*), but also many written and/ or produced by Argento such as *Demons* (*Dèmoni*, Lamberto Bava, 1985), *Demons 2* (*Dèmoni 2*, Lamberto Bava, 1986), *The Church* (*La chiesa*, Michele Soavi, 1989) and *The Sect* (*La Setta*, Michele Soavi, 1991). Argento has noted, however, that editing *Suspiria* was a relatively easy task simply because the decision to use rare film stock (a vital aspect of the film's production history that will be discussed further shortly) meant there was not a huge amount of material to edit: by one account, 14 weeks of filming resulted in only a few hundred metres of film.[40]

Cinematographer Luciano Tovoli is without question one of *Suspiria*'s key creative personnel, and is in large part responsible for its signature visual style. That being said, in every interview I have read with him, Tovoli has gone to great lengths to emphasise that he was very much under Argento's command. He makes it perfectly clear that the film is the result of Argento's vision, one that gave him space to indulge in his own creative and technical experiments that resulted in the film's trademark visual aesthetic. When he met Argento, Tovoli was known primarily for his work on Michelangelo Antonioni's *The Passenger* (1975). His early inspirations from the field of photography were Edward Weston, Ansel Adams and Henri Cartier-Bresson, and he studied classic neo-realist cinema closely to learn its technical mechanics. During the early stages of his career, realism was like a religion to Tovoli and naturalistic light became a fundamental element in the development of his own style of cinematic realism.

Devoted as Tovoli was to realist aesthetics, he and Argento may have initially seemed strange bedfellows. At the time of their first meeting, Tovoli knew of Argento by reputation already. He tells a charming story of living between two cinemas in Rome, and hearing screaming one evening outside his window. When investigating further, he discovered people were leaving one cinema where an Argento film was playing and then running to the other to watch it again. Although he had very little interest in horror at this stage, Tovoli told Stanley Manders, 'a director who provokes such brisk movement in a crowd should be a very good one!'[41]

For his part, Argento had a clear idea of the kind of colour and lighting he wanted for *Suspiria*. Turning to cinematographer Luigi Kuveiller with whom he had collaborated on both *Deep Red* and *The Five Days*, Argento showed him Disney's *Snow White and the Seven Dwarfs* to demonstrate the kind of visual intensity he was after. Disheartened by Kuveiller's lack of enthusiasm and inability to grasp the full potential of his vision, he went to Tovoli. While Argento knew almost immediately that Tovoli was the right person for the job, the cinematographer still admits some confusion as to why the director was so determined he join him on the project.

In an interview with Alan Jones, Tovoli said he told Argento that while the idea of making a Gothic fairy tale was of interest to him, he would prefer to do some technical tests in his own time to see if they were on the same wavelength. They were. After Argento's positive response, Tovoli agreed to work on the project and quickly assembled his crew: Camera Operator Idelmo Simonelli, First Camera Assistant Peppino Tinelli, Grip Mario Moreschini, and Gaffer Alberto Altibrandi. The spirit of experimentation that marked Tovoli's preliminary meetings with Argento were only amplified the further their collaboration developed. Relishing the director's encouragement that he use *Suspiria* as a forum to push his own creative and technical skills to their limits, Tovoli's often non-traditional methods sometimes surprised even his closest colleagues. For example, his extremely sharp backgrounds were the result of a painstaking construction of lights and mirrors: rather than using direct light on his subjects, Tovoli bounced lights into mirrors in varying distances from his subjects. Despite his earlier dedication to naturalism, *Suspiria*'s expressionist style allowed Tovoli scope to experiment with colour. Determined not to use coloured gels, filters or diffusers, Tovoli constructed frames of coloured tissue papers and velours through which he shone bright Arc lights to get the film's uniquely textured, dense colours. Tovoli has joked that if the actors look scared in the film, it is because they had reasonable concerns they might get burned because the lights were so close to their faces.

More famous, however, is Tovoli and Argento's use of film stock. Shot on what was even then hard-to-find Eastman 5254 colour negative stock and printed on an old-fashioned three-strip Technicolor printer, it was the last film in the world to be dye transferred. Carolo Labella and the Technicolour technicians who worked on *Suspiria* split the negative into three separate black and white negatives, each granted a specific colour: red, blue, and green. These were printed on top of each other, with the film's contrast amplified to further add to the intensity of its colours. *Suspiria* is a landmark film for reasons other than its use of Technicolor, however: amongst other things, it was one of the first (possibly the first) Italian films to utilise the recently launched Steadicam.

To privilege these visual qualities of *Suspiria* however ignores one of the film's most vital components: its soundtrack. Stephen Thrower has called *Suspiria* Argento's 'first instrumental work',[42] and the centrality of music to the film is nowhere better articulated than in Argento's own observation that 'rhythm is the key to anguish'.[43] Pushing the limits on *Suspiria*'s soundtrack as much as he did its visual elements, one of the film's many significant points of honour is its approach stereo sound. For cinemas lacking the updated equipment to play the four-track magnetic stereo soundtrack that was attached to the print, Argento opted for a less technologically advanced (but equally effective) alternative: in these cases, the film's score was pumped out into cinemas through a sound system placed behind the screen itself.

The importance of the soundtrack was rooted in the project long before its exhibition. Legend holds that the now legendary *Suspiria* soundtrack by prog rock band Goblin – with whom Argento had already collaborated with tremendous success on *Deep Red* – was played at maximum volume on the *Suspiria* set to create a suitably intense and unnerving ambience for the cast. While it is true that Goblin were played on set, however, the music that the cast heard was not the final soundtrack as it appears in the film. According to Goblin's Claudio Simonetti, they received the film's script from Argento before filming began, in the hope that the soundtrack could be done before he started shooting. Instead, what they produced was a preliminary musical sketch of tones and impressions, and it was *this* that was played while the film was shot. The final soundtrack was substantially different from this initial music, influenced heavily by the film's final unique look.

In terms of the direction that final soundtrack took, the Goblin score was conceived in a similar manner to that of *Deep Red*. In an interview with Alan Jones, Simonetti described casual listening parties where Argento and band members would listen to prog rock bands like Genesis and Emerson, Lake and Palmer. While the successful *Deep Red* soundtrack was ultimately a happy accident (by one account, it topped the Italian pop charts and had a place in the Top 40 for an entire year), Simonetti claimed the *Suspiria* soundtrack – an album he identified as the best thing the band ever did – was the result of a conscious, deliberate creative strategy.

Although they released earlier material as Cherry Five, it was Argento's search for musicians to perform in *Deep Red* that made Goblin's reputation. Despite that film already having a completed soundtrack by jazz composer Giorgio Gaslini (who had provided the soundtrack to Antonioni's 1961 film *The Night*), so impressed was Argento with Goblin that he asked them to create an alternative soundtrack, resulting in him keeping only three of Gaslini's pieces. Assuming Goblin was linked specifically to *Deep Red*, the band initially split, but with the success of the film and soundtrack in Italy they reformed and toured. They recorded their second album *Roller* in 1976 (which formed the basis of the soundtrack for George A. Romero's *Martin* in 1978), before reuniting once again with Argento to work on *Suspiria*.

Influences on Goblin's soundtrack for *Suspiria* have been identified across a broad spectrum, from Bernard Hermann's music for Alfred Hitchcock's *Psycho* (1960) through to the experimental approach to vocal effects in *The Exorcist* (William Friedkin, 1973). But the *Suspiria* soundtrack – like the film itself – is something uniquely its own, despite wearing its influences proudly on its sleeve. For Howard Hughes, it is 'one of the great horror scores, a web of sound – at one moment delicate folk music, the next a clattering dustbin lid din'. It is, he continues, 'a kaleidoscopic, cacophonous sound collage, resembling the depths of a torture chamber set to music'.[44]

And of course, the soundtrack is where the answer to the film's central enigma is first revealed: hidden in plain sound rather than sight, the track 'Witch' belts out during the film's opening sequence, the word repeated mantra-like, revealing *Suspiria*'s secret before we've arrived at the school. As the next chapter explores, however, the film is packed with equally playful tricks, both conceptual and formal. In *Suspiria*, magic is everywhere.

CHAPTER TWO: MEET DEATH NOW — WATCHING *SUSPIRIA*

If any horror film has gone out of its way to grab your attention in its opening moments, surely none have done so with quite the aplomb of *Suspiria*. Alan Jones has called 'the opening twenty minutes… the purest waking nightmare in the entire Argento canon if not the history of horror film',[45] and it is fully deserving of such praise. The film eschews any real attempt to establish a status quo for its story to deviate from, and drops both its protagonist and audience in an overwhelming maelstrom of sights and sounds. A frenzy of erratic, furious drums explode with Bernard Hermann-like shrieking strings, and white title credits burst onto a black screen. 'Suzy Bannion decided to perfect her ballet studies in the most famous school of dance in Europe', a male voiceover announces. 'She chose the celebrated academy of Freiburg'. The business-like tone of voice that launches the movie (spoken by Argento himself in the Italian-language version) mocks our reliance upon the need for normative grounding as its mentioning of specific times and places are immediately recognised as superfluous: 'One day at nine in the morning, she left Kennedy airport, New York, and arrived in Germany at 10:40 pm, local time.' Before the film has even really begun, it already joyfully brandishies its contradictions: the invitation into a 'once upon a time' whimsical fairy tale promise of its narrator's introduction is undermined by the data-based specifics of Suzy's arrival and departure details.

The voice is also distinctly masculine, noteworthy in a film that about the plurality of women's voices and stories. Suzy's arrival is a farewell to dominant masculinity. This symbolically disembodied male delivers data and then vanishes: there is no place for his voice here. While Argento's voiceover may be seen as an attempt at authorial control, that it is ultimately so out-of-place in *Suspiria*'s sensory frenzy can just as readily be seen as a simultaneous (and conscious) *debunking* of the director's ability to keep a handle on what is about to unfurl before us: *Suspiria* is at once both carefully crafted and thoroughly out of control.

The voiceover is overtaken by the return of pounding drums, effectively drowning out the voice of masculine reason, and acting as a warning that the logic of language will soon be obscured and defeated by more sensory, corporeal experiences. Diegetic spikes

Suzy arrives at the Munich airport

and dips in volume merge with the first whispers of the famous music box motif, as the soundtrack mimics Suzy's experience of the sound outside from the tumultuous world beyond the airport doors. Shot on location at the Munich airport, the site of Suzy's arrival is aggressively defamiliarised, drenched in a bright red light. Alighting from their flight, Suzy and her fellow travellers leave a realm of comparatively naturalistic lighting as they enter the airport's foyer. Unlike her fellow passengers (including Daria Nicolodi in a brief cameo), Suzy's presence is emphasized by a white outfit that suddenly glows pink. Chameleon-like, the innocence that white traditionally signifies in this instance mark her physically as susceptible to her environment. In fact, the development of Suzy's strength to resist the influence of her environment is central to the film's plot. A brief flash of the airport's arrival and departures board is shown, bathed in a toxic green: the world of logic, with its words and numbers, is both mocked and polluted through this tonal stain.

Much has been made of the close-up of the airport's automatic door as Suzy walks through it. Intense shifts in the colour palate and changes in the soundtrack privilege Suzy's exit from the airport. A portal into another dimension, the sliding door is is one of the first passageways that Suzy will discover during her adventures in Germany. After crossing this initial threshold, the world outside explodes around her. As she enters the rain, Suzy's clothes and hair swirl around her as if pulled in different directions by external forces beyond her control. Struggling with her luggage, the rain, and her attempt to hail a taxi, she finds herself in a situation totally out of control. Even at this early stage of the film, invisible external forces are aligning to warn both her and the audience of things to come.

Crucially, however, some elements from the 'real' world remain. Most curious of these is the blink-and-you'll-miss-it-flash of a row of golden arches, the internationally recognisable McDonalds logo. Like the appearance of Munich's BMW Headquarters later in the film, these multinational corporate icons do not stand for the intrusion of reality into *Suspiria*'s dark fantasy, but rather signify the corruption and greed that underscore coven leader Helena Markos' occult dominion. As is later made explicit, the coven's ultimate desire is for financial wealth through the suffering of others.

This tension between the real and the fantastic manifested in more practical terms during shooting: after attempting to shoot the external airport sequence three times in the rain, Argento realised that rain machines produced a far more convincing shower. If Suzy was hoping for respite within the taxi, she fails to find it. The driver is gruff to the point of hostility, and already having refused to help her with her luggage, he seems to antagonize her with his refusal to correctly identify her instructions (even though she pronounces the address in the same way he does). Again, the dominance of language is challenged in the world of *Suspiria*. Played by Argento regular Fulvio Mingozzi, his role as the taxi driver – who James Gracey has identified as a kind of 'ferryman figure, transporting the damned to their dark destinations'[46] – would later be revamped in *Inferno*. This is not the only important cameo in Suzy's taxi ride towards the ballet school, however: the reflection of Argento himself appears briefly as the screaming face Suzy sees in the dividing window that separates her and the driver.

The legacy of Mario Bava – particularly in *The Whip and the Body* (1963), *Black Sabbath* (1963) and *Kill Baby, Kill* (1966) – all come to the fore during Suzy's taxi ride, drenched in rich, dark jewel colours. Adrian Horrocks draws a link between visual poetics of how Suzy is shot in this sequence and stained glass imagery of the Madonna,[47] a perfect point of reference for a character who radiates innocence in a world that is anything but. *Suspiria*'s art historical influences do not end here, and the entire film is marked by a painter's sense of composition. As cinematographer Luciano Tovoli told Alan Jones, 'everything is in *Suspiria*, from Romanticism and Renaissance art to Impressionism and Surrealism. I would be lying if I said that was my overall aim, but that's the final result nevertheless'.[48]

The internal taxi shots introduced what would be Tovoli's strategy for the film's use of colour, where primary and complementary colours throb across its surfaces. Just as striking as the imagery in *Suspiria*'s opening scenes, however, is Goblin's intoxicating soundtrack. This lullaby-run-amuck pulsates across Tovoli's lush visuals, a frenzy of the aural as much as it is the visible. The secret that elides Suzy throughout her adventures in the film's netherworld are revealed here from the outset, the word 'witch!' repeated time and time again as Suzy is trundled across Munich towards the cursed ballet school. The sense of terror in *Suspiria*'s opening is embedded in its soundtrack as much as it is in anything we see or are told: its pounding beats drum terror into our heads more effectively than anything our intellects could attempt to fathom.

Weaving through the dark, wet streets of night-time Munich, visual motifs that will flood the film until its final moments begin to appear: roads become winding, mysterious corridors, and trees, grates, and columns form bars and grids that lock its characters within the confines of *Suspiria*'s horrors. If Suzy's journey towards the Tanzakademie has been intense, nothing could prepare her – or us – for the aggressive luridness of the building itself. That it simultaneously looks so unreal yet is based on a real building – the Haus Zum Walfisch in Freiburg im Breisgau (now Baden-Württemberg), painstakingly replicated in a Rome film studio – undermines *Suspiria*'s fascination with the lines that supposedly distinguish reality from fantasy. With its bright red façade, the Tanzakademie is drenched in the same red as the airport. Thus far, Germany has been all flesh and blood.

Presented with the riddle that will drive her quest through the film – what did Pat HIngle say at the door as she left the Tanzakademie? – soggy Suzy is turned away in the rain, and returns to her cab to find alternate accommodation for the evening. As she drives into the night, there are echoes of Tom Gunning's 'cinema of attractions', underscoring *Suspiria*'s self-awareness of its own spectacular legacy. Alan Jones' has cited a contemporary review of the film by Giovanni Grazzini that notes how it 'goes back to cinema's roots in the Fantastic, using sound and colour with a cleverness that's truly remarkable'.[49] James Gracey has drawn a parallel between early cinema traditions and this sequence where Suzy looks out her taxi window to see Pat running through the dense, black-and-white pinstriped forest, comparing it to a zoetrope.[50]

Leaving Suzy, the film's first – and most famous – murder vignette begins. Argento has often said that he wanted to begin *Suspiria* with the kind of intensity that would end other horror films in order to leave the audience wondering what could possibly follow. Arriving at her friend Sonia's (Susanna Javicoli), these characters ultimately have little to do with the plot, and Argento's privileging of their demise pertains more to spectacle than to narrative development. If there is one sequence in the film that stands above the others in terms of impact, formal construction, creative zeal and conceptual audacity, this is it. The emphasis on sharp lines and geometric shapes stand in direct contrast to the soft curves and bloody blurs of female bodies that will soon explode across its surfaces.

After the sensory whirlwind that marked Suzy's introduction to Germany, Pat's arrival at Sonia's apartment initially suggests Argento is allowing the audience a moment to catch their breath as the girls chat quietly in a pastel-hued room. This tranquillity is short lived, as Pat's face is smashed through a bathroom window by a pair of black leather gloved hand (another Argento cameo) after she sees an ominous pair of glowing eyes spying at her from outside. Stabbed through the heart, the camera zooms into a gore shot that is again both real and unreal: wearing its construction on its sleeve by removing the context of Pat's body that supposedly surrounds the organ, the horror of this shot stems less from its verisimilitude than its brazenness. While tempting to focus solely on the glamorized erotics that Argento brings to this sequence, as Stephen Thrower has indicated, there is a crucial interplay at work here fundamental to Argento's broader aesthetic vision:

> ...whilst the image of the beating heart of a screaming woman being penetrated by a knife borders on the pornographic, there's something alien and unerotic – and important – about the degree of theatricality that's been expended to get us there. It's in the tension between the erotic indulgence of sadism and its flamboyant exaggeration into artifice that Argento wields his distinctive sense of style.[51]

Flung through the stained glass ceiling in the building's foyer – shattering the logic of its geometric shapes, exploding the cosmic order that art history's focus on the sacred has so long fought to maintain – the camera pans down Pat's hanging corpse until it hits the ground, working its way over Sonia's bloody body, impaled by the wreckage that has fallen from above.

The offer of peace *Suspiria* tempts us with when Pat first arrived at Sonia's apartment is finally granted after this gruelling murder as Suzy arrives at the Tanzakademie the next morning. In one of the film's rare external daytime shots, Suzy looks off camera as she arrives, smiling in the sun as the blind piano player Daniel and his dog walk in before her:

a playful metaphor for the blind leading the blind. Inside the building, police investigate Pat and Sonia's murder. Key characters are also introduced: Alida Valli's Miss Tanner is played with what Xavier Mendick has described perfectly as an 'authoritarian zeal',[52] Alan Brien calling her a 'Nazified dance teacher, with a rat-trap smile'.[53] Throughout the film there is a distinct yet indefinable hint of lesbianism to Tanner, as there is also to Joan Bennett's gravel-voiced Madam Blanc. Here she is draped in an outfit both age-inappropriate (emphasised by her heavy make-up) and anachronistic (recalling, perhaps, Bennett's background in Classical Hollywood cinema), rendering her otherwise cool, calm and in-control persona oddly eerie. In one of the film's funniest moments, Miss Tanner introduces the creepy Pavlo (Giuseppe Transocchi) – 'he speaks only Romanian', she says - mocking his gingivitis and openly calling him ugly, paying little heed to Suzy's clear discomfort in the impressively awkward situation. The scene also introduces memorable minor characters such as Albert, Mark and Olga as they hover in the background.

The colour palette is now dominated by blue, black, white and gold, providing another dislocating contrast: there are almost no reds here, a colour that so aggressively marked the opening murder sequence. The skewed angles of a large fake window recall German Expressionism, and loom above a stairwell whose bannister look like coiled golden snakes. In the background, the red oesophageal corridors of the Tanzakademie can be seen, emphasising associations between the building and the human body. The snake-like stairwell foreshadows the viper's nest Suzy finds herself in as she meets the other students in the Tanzakademie's dressing room – the deliciously vampy Olga (Barbara Magnolfi) makes this explicit as she tells Suzy and her new friend Sarah (Stefania Casini) 'I once read that names which begin with the letter "S" are the names of *snakes!*' After her already overwhelming arrival in Germany, the behaviour of her peers as they squabble over money makes Sarah's kindness a visible relief to Suzy. But it is Olga's apartment where she finds herself that evening after Madam Blanc has explained to her that her original plan to live on-campus is not possible.

Olga's apartment provides yet another visual shock, as it is almost completely drained of colour in stark contrast to the hyperactive primary palette that has marked the film visually thus far. But what its black and white colour scheme lacks in saturated hues it makes up for in intricately detailed *mise en scene*, a confident and elaborate *horror vacui*.

Its busy monochromatic wallpaper surrounds Olga as she gossips on the telephone, her elaborately bunned hair mimicking the blooms on the surrounding walls. Mark (Miguel Bosè) is fleetingly presented as a potential love interest for Suzy. The inclusion of this never-expanded plotline underscores the futility of men in *Suspiria*: Suzy doesn't need him, and we don't need the kind of romantic storyline his character's inclusion would traditionally bring. Suzy has more important things on her mind, as she tries to recall precisely what she heard Pat say on the evening of her and Sonia's murder.

Suzy reflects in Olga's apartment

Returning to the Tanzakademie, Suzy warms up, but in the action that follows her presence here is marked by her *not* dancing. This will become a continuing irony in what is effectively a film about a ballet school that includes almost no dancing. Rather, it replaces the traditional notion of choreography with horror's perverse subversion of it, as its victims' bodies offer a corrupted variation of corporeal performativity. Walking through a rich dark red velvet curtain, Miss Tanner's arrival is literally framed by her connection to the pulsating, body-like Tanzakademie itself: soon after her barked demand that dancers proceed to their class, Suzy has her first run-in with Madam Blanc when she refuses to move into the Tanzakademie residence, preferring instead to stay with Olga. Complimenting Suzy on her strong will, Miss Tanner's praise ominously foreshadows a bleak turn of events.

In one of the film's most memorable sequences, Suzy *jetés* into a long red corridor. Students exit at the other end, and in the centre sits a kitchen hand polishing silver, as Albert stands to her side and looks on. Goblin's soundtrack increases in intensity as Suzy hesitantly approaches them, terrified and fascinated in equal measure. The kitchen hand carefully lifts the sharp blade she is polishing up to a beam of light, dazzling Suzy as specks of dust turn to glitter. The very second the light hits Suzy's eyes, Albert breaks into an intense grin, empowered by her trauma – it is as if the energy is being sucked out through the light into him, a notion further enforced by the fact that his smile vanishes the second the beam of light dies out.

Bewitching Suzy

Magic is everywhere in *Suspiria*, but is perhaps nowhere as strong or as incomprehensibly powerful as it is in this short sequence. There is no explanation given for how this gesture brings Suzy under the witches' control. But this it does, and she stumbles woozily don the corridor. Entering the Yellow Room for her first class, Miss Tanner insists she dance but Suzy collapses after a token wobble, her nose and mouth bleeding. In another red corridor, girls gather around her door and Madam Blanc assists Miss Tanner in forcing Suzy to drink water. Quietly, the kitchen hand puts Suzy's clothes into the room's wardrobe – fulfilling Madam Blanc's earlier request, Suzy must now live at the Tanzakedemie. Injected by a mysterious drug, the doctor recommends Suzy rest and prescribes her red wine. Her confusion is compounded as much by the strange events as they are by the kaleidoscope of colours that surround her as light pours into the room via multi-coloured stained glass windows.

Unable to join her fellow students girls for the evening meal, Suzy is transfixed by the mirror in her room, hypnotised by the collision of the real and the unreal in her strange new home. Framed by the different shapes and colours of Suzy's bedroom, her and Sarah chat about the unusual goings-on at their dance school, until Pavlo interrupts them and silently admires Sarah's cigarette lighter. Bathed in a red, Suzy is left alone in her room, and combing her hair welcomes another of the film's more memorable sequences. The room is suddenly flooded with a dark blue light, and intercutts between her and Sarah's room as the girls fuss with their hair, discovering squirming maggots that have fallen from the ceiling.

Author of the indispensible *Massacred by Mother Nature: Exploring the Natural Horror Film* (2012) and regular *Fangoria* magazine writer Lee Gambin has particular insight into the role of animals in horror film, and emphasises the significance of the maggots in *Suspiria*. 'Witches have always been associated with bugs and insects, and the biggest insult in that realm would be the vile maggot,' he says. 'This repugnant creature that is attracted to the dead or to the rotten pops up in *Suspiria* as an indication that this ballet academy is not entirely a place of wholesome activity.' He continues: 'It is a beautiful play on reported turn of the century practices of witchcraft where Satan-worshipping women (and men) would cause it to rain frogs or serpents.'[54]

Goblin's soundtrack underscores the chaos and panic as terrified students rush into the red hallway out of rooms of equally vivid jewel colours. Miss Tanner takes charge, discovering a box of maggot-infested meat in the attic, emphasising the existence of something literally rotten at work within the Tanzakedemie's walls. Slow motion zooms into the writhing creatures emphasise Argento's pleasure in these kinds of visceral gross-outs, and he plays this repulsion aspect as long as he can sustain it.

A dramatic shift in tone finds a number of students and staff in Madam Blanc's office. Sitting or standing, all figures are female except for the notably effeminate Albert, whose centrality in the shot's composition indicates his privileged place in the Tanzakedemie's hierarchy. Positioned in a circle in Madam Blanc's round office with the powerful woman standing in front and centre of her altar-like desk, the scene's *mise en scene* evokes a crucial sense of ritual. The lines between the fantastic and reality are again exposed as diegetically unstable, as the garden mural on the walls – and the all-important irises – is contrasted with large potted plants that litter the room.

Above Suzy's head on the wall is a conspicuous print featuring a detail from Aubrey Beardsley's 'John and Salome' (1894), one of the illustrations created by the British artist to accompany the first print edition of Oscar Wilde's play *Salome* that same year. There are many ways to approach the inclusion of Beardsley's work here: on one hand, it may simply be a case that Argento liked it and it stylistically suited the scene. But its strategic placement above Suzy's head implies its meaning may run deeper. The omission of John the Baptist that appeared in the original, for example, implies a conscious eradication of both the masculine and the sacred, leaving only monstrous femininity in its wake.

Signficantly positioned near Suzy, it is a warning to her, but one that she cannot see as her she is facing the other way.

Madam Blanc explains to the students and staff that an order of meat had turned, causing the infestation of maggots. She tells them that a temporary dormitory will be established, and staff and the few male students busy themselves hanging white sheets (for privacy?) and set up cots for the girls to sleep in overnight. The sheets – notable for their visual blandness in such a hypersaturated movie – literally set a stage for a performance, and as the overhead lights are turned out and a dark red light floods the space, their function becomes visible: they become the canvas for one of *Suspiria*'s most famous images, as the silhouette of The Directress herself is shown sleeping behind the draped sheets. Recalling Lotte Reninger's iconic animated fairy tale *The Adventures of Prince Achmed* (1926), this scene echoes the traditions of shadow puppetry, again linking *Suspiria*'s to pre-cinematic moving picture making forms. As Suzy and Sarah whisper conspiratorially in their prim nightgowns, spooked by the presence of the eerie, snoring Directress, Argento's intention of creating a world that mirrors the wild imagination of children becomes even more apparent.

*Suzy and Sarah
in the temporary
dormitory*

There is another dramatic shift in tone as the film cuts to daytime. The early scene of Suzy and Daniel arriving at the school is replicated, although this time Suzy is notably absent: she now lies within its walls, no longer an outsider. Leaving his German Shepard at the door, Daniel enters the building, but the slow zoom into his canine companion foreshadows its ominous role. In a brief but crucial exchange, Miss Tanner is revealed to be a liar when Sarah asks her on the stairwell if the Directress slept in the Tanzakademie on the previous evening and is told this was not the case.

Outside, the kitchen hand and Albert approach the building hesitantly. The dog looks up and growls, but the attack on Albert that Miss Tanner soon accuses it of is not shown: rather, the camera pans slowly down the very corridor where Suzy was bewitched by the kitchen hand and Albert earlier in the film. Why? It is certainly not the case that Argento is squeamish; this has already been established with gusto. Rather, perhaps showing the child as a victim would risk aligning the viewer with Albert, challenging the carefully – although very subtle – construction of him as a indefinably malevolent force. Or would any display of the dog's tendency towards violence detract from the impact of his upcoming attack on his owner? Alternatively – and most tantalizingly – is the possibility that the attack never happened at all. We only have the second hand report of Miss Tanner that the dog did in fact attack Albert. Did the witches sense that the dog had an insight into their true identities, an insight that the film's human protagonists have thus far been blind to?

The confrontation between Miss Tanner and Daniel in the Yellow Room shatters yet another potential moment where this film about a ballet school might in fact show some dancing. Banging her fist on the piano, Tanner and the piano player pull no punches, and Daniel tells her that he has a greater idea of what is going on at the Tanzakedemie than they might think he does. Furious but laughing, Daniel makes the important declaration as he leaves the school that he can finally smell fresh air: again, another explicit reference to the rot that riddles the institution, both literally and metaphorically.

Suzy is still begrudgingly eating her meals alone in her room. Drugged and drowsy, she struggles to follow Sarah's train of thought as she describes the strange goings on in the academy at night. As Sarah counts the mysterious footsteps of the ladies of the academy as they go about their mysterious evening business, a close up of high heels walking down a corridor is shown, accompanied by the evocative tap-tap-tapping sound as they hit the hardwood floor. Flooded with red and then dark blue light, there is a *film noir* quality to these two brief but important close-ups, as again dangerous femininity is rendered explicit.

These wandering shots take over as the camera floats, seemingly governed by some unseen supernatural force throughout the corridors of the academy. In one brief but crucial moment, a tutu is shown, lit by a beam of bright white light, conspicuous amongst the dark blues and reds that otherwise dominate this sequence. Its ornate, jewelled bodice and the burst of tulle that hovers beneath are eerily disembodied, a ghostly reminder of the notable absence of dance. As Sarah explains to the bewildered Suzy, the staff of the Tanzakedemie have other things on their mind. Returning again to the corridor where the spell was cast on Suzy, the wind gives motion to a golden curtain that adds further credence to the sense that the building is alive and pulsing, tucked away as it is behind the rib-like arches that run along it.

In one of the film's most exquisite transitions, this disembodied and ethereal camera lands on a shot of the moon, denoting the cosmic omnipresence of the mystical forces that the Tanzakedemie's witches seek to control. This power is about to be displayed with excessive, violent force as we arrive in a traditional Munich *bierkeller*. Lederhosen-clad men dance joyfully, oblivious to the monstrous feminine power that surrounds them. Daniel leaves the bar and makes the grave error of taking a night-time walk through Munich's infamous Königsplatz. Karl von Fischer's design for the square was inspired by Greece's Acropolis when he conceived it in the nineteenth century in honour of Crown Prince Ludwig of Bavaria. Despite today being the city's cultural hub, it has a far less pleasant history due to the predilection of the Nazis for the space: the huge rallies that marked the Third Reich were regularly housed here. The pro-Hitler Youth propaganda film *The March to the Führer* (1940) includes footage of Königsplatz during this era, and the Nazis built a number of buildings in the area, many of which were destroyed by the US Army in the late 1940s. A number of critics have noted the significance of this history to *Suspiria*. James Gracey has questioned if the director was 'aligning the evil and oppression of the three mothers with that of the Nazis',[55] while Julian Horrocks suggests the scene is 'a comment on fascism… [where] the blind man is a representation of Italy, his dog the beguiled Mussolini, and the bird German fascism'.[56] Linda Schulte-Sasse expands these readings even further, emphasising that Miss Tanner is herself notably Germanic, 'an allusion to the sadistic, Lina Wertmuelleresque, Nazi female guard', and that Daniel's dog is a German Shepard (an explicit link to the SS).[57]

As Lee Gambin has also noted, the significance of the dog in this scene is intrinsic to its horror and relies on a long cultural history of how this particular animal has been represented and understood in the arts. For Gambin,

The dog's violent reaction stems from either being completely afraid of the menace that surrounds and as a response to this impeding threat but it could also be read as being an attack made under the influence of the malevolence surrounding the ballet academy. There is no real reason as to why this loyal German Shepard tears his master's throat out, he is just doing what he feels he has to in fear that his handicapped human companion may be seduced or influenced by the evils that surround the dance school. Or, much like the Rottweilers in *The Omen* (1976) or the ambassador for Satan himself in the form of a fellow German Shepherd in *Devil Dog: Hound of Hell* (1978), the dog could also be reacting as an extension of the evils of this prestigious institution run by witches.

He continues:

> In horror film and literature, dogs have been either the protectors of the innocent … and yet have also been depicted as agents of evil and the soldiers of Satan. However, here in Argento's excursion into witchcraft, the dog's aggressive attack comes as a complete surprise and can be read both ways – as a defender of the good and a precautionary protector or as a canine under the influence.

As one of the most memorable scenes of violence in the whole film, Daniel's death is notable for how it deviates from the rest of the movie. It is for one thing a rare external shot: aside from Daniel and Suzy's arrivals and her upcoming meeting with Dr Mandel and Professor Milius, it is one of the few sequences that does not occur in controlled, internal space. More overtly, it also replaces Tovoli's saturated colours with a monochromatic black and white, allowing a privileged saturation of colour only to emphasise the visceral spectacle of Daniel's blood and sinew.

Offering a moment of relief after Daniel's graphic murder, Suzy listens with concern as Olga and another student discuss Daniel's death. Increasingly lost in her own reflection, it is through Suzy that the film seemingly appears to be questioning the veracity of the real and the unreal as the camera zooms in slowly to the reflection of her face in the mirror in the room's grid-like décor. Suddenly seated at Madam Blanc's desk, another mirror appears behind Suzy showing Miss Tanner appearing from the corridor, lined with dark red arabesque wallpaper. Again, the Beardsley image – powerful, violent Salome with the notable omission of John the Baptist – is placed beside this reflected image of

Miss Tanner. Madam Blanc asks Miss Tanner to leave, and Suzy voices her concerns about Pat's death. She mentions that she heard the girl say the words 'secret' and 'irises' as their paths crossed. Just like the Goblin soundtrack in the opening moments that whispered the revelation of the Tanzakedemie's supposed secret – *witch!* – again, the answers to *Suspiria*'s mysteries are hidden in plain view: positioned between Suzy and Madam Blanc on the wall behind them are the three irises so important to Suzy's final revelation of the Tanzakademie's dark mysteries.

In Madam Blanc's office

Suspiria is proud of its influences, and these are nowhere as explicit than in the scene where Suzy and Sarah go swimming at the Munich bathhouse. Argento has acknowledged the films of Val Lewton at RKO in the 1940s as an influence on his work, and this sequence is an effective love letter to what was arguably Lewton's most successful collaboration with Jacques Tourneur, *Cat People* (1942). Filmed on location in Munich's glorious art nouveau *Müller'sches Volksbad*, the building was gifted to the city by engineer Karl Müller. His only condition was that it was to be a pool for the poor, opening its doors in 1901 at a time when private bathrooms were a rarity. This democratic spirit of the space's utility is openly perverted by the indefinable presence of some kind of supernatural entity as – recalling *Cat People* – the camera flies and floats above the girls. This implies an ominous first person glimpse of Suzy and Sarah in what they otherwise believe to be a private moment, engrossed as they are in their discussions concerning the strange events plaguing the Tanzakedemie.

Returning to the dance school, increasingly skewed external shots mark the growing power of the building and the witches housed within. Suzy's apparently drugged food and wine glows a menacing red as she slumbers in the background, the frantic Sarah unable to rouse her. Sarah is drenched in a noxious green light, marked by the witches toxicity. Realising she is now alone as Suzy woozily collapses back in a stupor, Sarah wanders terrified through the Tanzakedemie's corridors, her terror brought to life through the merciless pounding of the Goblin score as much as by the unseen by powerful presence of the supernatural. Greens give way to reds and blues as she leaves Suzy's bedroom, the American girl stirring slightly with the unconscious knowledge that something dreadful is about to befall her friend.

Formally, Sarah is assaulted as much by light, colour and music as she is by the demonic force that eventually catches up with her. Running from room to room, she fights valiantly for survival. But a close up of a switchblade being removed from a case in a shot reminiscent of *Deep Red* – note also here two pearl-ended pins that will make a grotesque re-appearance in the dead Sarah's eyes in the films climax – implies that her demise will both be lengthy and unpleasant. Sarah is impeded not only by the murderous force that chases her through the school, but by random and at times absurd additions to the *mise en scene*, such as falling into a room filled with wire that traps the struggling, desperate girl. Despite her efforts, Sarah is defeated, and again it is Argento's own hand that appears in the black leather glove that slashes the doomed dance student's throat.

Even for those who know the film intimately, *Suspiria* still has its surprises. James Gracey is the author of Kamera Books' *Dario Argento* (2010), a rigorous work that demonstrates an encyclopaedic knowledge of the director's ouvre. But, Gracey says, even he can discover things he's never noticed before; 'I love the idea that there are things skulking throughout the shadows of this otherwise lividly lit nightmare of a film'. He continues:

This idea was confirmed last year [2013] when the Belfast Film Festival screened *Suspiria*, with a live soundtrack courtesy of Claudio Simonetti and the Simonetti Horror Project, and I caught a glimpse of something I'd never seen before, despite having seen *Suspiria* so many times. Isn't it magical when that happens? I attribute this to seeing the film on a big screen. The aforementioned moment came during the scene when Sarah makes her bid for escape after failing to awaken a heavily drugged Suzy. She is stalked through the impossibly structured spaces of the school and up into the labyrinthine attic. She moves through pools of ominously pulsating light and all-consuming darkness, into a nightmarish realm where every door leads her further into the shadows of Mater Suspiriorum's dank domain. She is eventually attacked by an unseen assailant brandishing a cut-throat razor. During previous viewings, her attacker is always too enshrouded in shadows to see clearly, but this time, there 'he' was; a dark, diabolical sentry with the same cat-like eyes as Pat's murderer. Catching sight of this witch's minion – just standing behind Sarah as she tiptoes down the hallway, quietly watching, waiting, and plotting bloody murder - was a creepy delight that not only sent icy chills down my spine, but completely reinvigorated my love for the film. Who knows what is still yet to be glimpsed for the first time in this classic witch-infested tale of the occult...[58]

In a rare and therefore conspicuous moment of naturalistic lighting, Suzy enters Sarah's bedroom and finds it hastily ransacked. Seeing things for how they really are for a brief moment, Suzy instantly understands that something untoward has happened to her friend, and is understandably suspicious of Miss Tanner's unconvincing explanation for Sarah's sudden disappearance. With nowhere else to turn, she calls Sarah's friend Dr Frank Mandel (Udo Kier) in the hope he has information, and arranges to meet him. As the truth about the Tanzakedemie is a revealed to her, the film formally mirrors an increasing sense of exposure and revelation: this is perhaps nowhere more apparent than the dramatic and sudden appearance of an external daytime scene, where Mandel and Suzy meet to discuss the events at the ballet school.

Filmed on location outside Munich's BMW Headquarters, the building – whose design mimics a car engine's four cylinders – is one of the city's most famous landmarks, its unveiling coinciding with the 1972 Olympic Games. Having appeared previously in Norman Jewison's dystopian sci-fi classic *Rollerball* (1975), the building here represents futuristic modernity, positioned in sharp contrast to the medieval superstitions that mark the Tanzakademie. A sign in the building's courtyard informs us that the building is housing the Sixth Meeting of New Studies in Psychiatry and Psychology, where Mandel provides a brief overview of the Tanzakedemie's history. He tells Suzy that Markos was a practicing witch known as The Black Queen. After being persecuted across Europe, she settled in Freiburg and established the school, specializing in ballet and occult studies. Dying in a fire in 1905, Markos was replaced as head of the school by a favoured student who apparently steered the institution towards a more legitimate sole focus on dance alone. His colleague Professor Milius expands further, informing

Suzy on the broader power of witches and their desire for wealth and the suffering of others. Significantly, he tells Suzy that the only way to destroy a coven is to kill its leader, comparing it to a cobra without a head. Young and handsome, Mandel initially represents a level-headed rationalism linked to the reason and modernity signified by their contemporary location. But Tovoli's camera begins to wander, seemingly compelled towards the astral plane as he shoots Mandel and Suzy from below with only the clouds as their backdrop.

Professor Milius tells Suzy about witches

Mandel's famous declaration that 'bad luck isn't brought by broken mirrors, but by broken minds' may be one of the film's most memorable moments of dialogue, but it is one promptly undone by Milius. Marked by both his authority over and generational difference to Mandel, he dismisses his colleague's rational explanation. A dramatic birds eye shot of the concrete courtyard in which the scene's action is taking place again implies an unseen, supernatural presence, reminding us of the ubiquitous and inescapable supernatural forces dominating the film's action. Captivated by Milius' bizarre story, the camera zooms slowly into his and Suzy's faces as the intensity of their conversation increases. The slide into the world of his shocking story is visually paired with a simultaneous increase in kaleidoscopic imagery, as the reflective windows behind them increasingly become the dominant focal point. Even the mere mention of the witches has the power to shatter the boundaries that distinguish reality from the fantastic. As the scene progresses, it is not Suzy and Milius we see, but their blurred reflections. Despite Mandel's previous claims, what we see before us *are* broken mirrors – glass in which we initially see a reflection, but then only shattered images. They are not broken minds at all.

Empowered by this newly discovered information, on her return to the Tanzakedemie

Suzy becomes increasingly suspicious of the contents of her food and wine. Realising that the other students have gone out for the evening, she promptly disposes of her tainted dinner. In one of the most playful images in the entire film, she pours her wine down the bathroom sink, but it is clearly of a consistency and colour that is not wine, but neither is it the blood that the splashes of red would otherwise imply. Rather, what Suzy pours down the sink – scrubbing it with her now-stained hands – is paint, subtly revealing what the more overt flamboyant elements of the film's construction have been knowingly acknowledging from its very first moments: that it is a construction.

Turning the bathroom light off, the intense colours again become dominant, and almost immediately herald the appearance of an ominous, supernatural omen. As a bat enters the room to attack Suzy, the girl flails her arms and struggles in a manner reminiscent of Tippi Hedren in Alfred Hitchcock's *The Birds* (1952), once again allowing associations to be made between the British director and Argento's reputation as the so-called 'Italian Hitchcock'. But this is a bat, rather than a bird, and as Lee Gambin has noted, 'bats have always been a staple of the horror film and most obviously connected to the legend of the vampire, however there are many films that employ the bat as a representation of the threat of death, the frantic and frenzied resurrection of a new life and as a reflection of inner-turmoil experienced by characters that populate the silver screen'. In *Suspiria*, Gambin notes that the bat 'informs Suzy that death is nigh, it is the catalyst for her change and development and it is a crazed insight into her mental and emotional state right from the beginning of the film'. Importantly, Gambin notes an intrinsically sexual quality to this sequence:

> Suzy becomes flustered, starts to breathe heavily, exerts herself physically and then finally lets go once she bashes the bat to death, leaving a blood stained white towel as the coda to her experience. The white towel being stained with blood is … a nice wink at her sexual awakening. The scene after Suzy kills the bat shows her having a cigarette (the mandatory post-sex smoke) and looking far less nervous and fragile as she has throughout the movie. From here on, Suzy takes charge and becomes the Nancy Drew of horror – marking her turf and making her way into horror heroine territory.[59]

That it is her sexually-coded run-in with the bat that marks Suzy's transition into an active, determined heroine is crucial. Argento himself has noted that *Suspiria* is in large part reliant on a deliberate and conscious linkage between the witches and lesbianism, and the metaphorical sexual awakening that Gambin identifies as underpinning the bat scene therefore functions as an essential moment in the development of Suzy's own sexual identity. Empowered and determined, Suzy now has the knowledge – both intellectually and physically – to allow her to confront the witches in the climax.

In line with *Suspiria*'s fairy tale tone, the act of tracing footsteps à la *Hansel and Gretel* becomes integral to Suzy's discovery of the witch's lair. Following Sarah's vaguely remembered instructions, she symbolically journeys through spaces stylistically marked by competing tones of naturalistic lighting and the film's until-now dominant palate of dark, jewel colours. Even as she tiptoes past the kitchen, the kitchen hand who had previously bewitched her is revealed in bright, naturalistic light, as she overzealously cuts meat. Running into the corridor where she first placed her ominous charm on Suzy, the kitchen hand is suddenly soaked in dark red light, but now it is she that cannot see. The tables are turned, and it is Suzy who is now in control.

Argento has noted in numerous interviews that he deliberately placed the Tanzakedemie's door knobs up high to imply the child-like quality of the dance students, and this is most obvious in the close up of Suzy entering Madam Blanc's office. With the four oval-shaped Beardsley prints lining the back wall as she walks towards the floral mural, Suzy is almost intuitively drawn to the Escher-like painting as the dark colours of the décor and Tovoli's lighting swirls around her. Establishing the power relations for the film's climactic showdown, Argento chooses not to show the witches themselves, but rather privileges images of the buildings exterior, standing firm in all its confident, late Gothic-era splendour. A close-up of a plaque near the doorway is an intriguing, tantalising inclusion at this moment. During the Renaissance, Hans Zum Walfisch was the residence of noted Christian humanist Desiderius Erasmus von Rotterdam (1469–1536), to whom the plaque is dedicated. There are potentially myriad ways to interpret this fact at this stage of the movie, but perhaps the most compelling emphasises this historical figures' notorious impartiality in the tensions that were brewing at the time between Martin Luther and the Catholic Church. Like the witches that now dwell within the building, there was an element of hubris to Erasmus' story: he believed his intellect and work would naturally endear him to the powerful and the elite, but his resistance to take a side ultimately angered many, including Luther himself. Markos and her followers' assumption that their power was absolute is – thanks to Suzy – also soon revealed as a serious misjudgement.

In Madam Blanc's office, the reflections that have haunted Suzy throughout the film now come to her aid, and it is via a mirror that her attention is first drawn to the coloured irises on the mural. A flashback to her encounter with Pat reminds her of the importance of the blue iris, a quick spin of which unlocks a door that grants her entry into a hidden corridor. Her journey down this corridor is one of the film's most baroque and beautiful images: a long arched corridor, with ornate black and gold paintings along their walls. Flooded with golden light cutting through the shadows, text in a multitude of different languages lines her path as she tentatively makes her way forward. Hearing voices, she sneaks past a room where she sees Madam Blanc and her followers for who they really are in a bright white light. Blanc demands Suzy's death, and again Albert is privileged in this brief shot, standing at her side and recalling a witch's familiar. A frenzy of interchanging jewel-coloured lighting shatters the scene as loyal servant Miss Tanner assists Madam Blanc in a corrupted ritual reminiscent of the Catholic Eucharist, confirming their evil subversions and explicitly revealing the source of their dark power.

Endowed with newfound power after this ceremony, Suzy shudders involuntarily as Madam Blanc's declaration that they must 'kill the American girl' begins to materialise. Recoiling backwards, Suzy discovers to her horror Sarah's corpse: if the placement of the pearl-ended pins that appeared earlier in the film in the dead girl's open, staring eyes aren't enough to terrify both Suzy and the audience, then the large nails pounded through her wrists in a mock crucifixion (another subversion of Catholicism) certainly complete the task. With little time to respond, Sarah rushes away from Pavlo – brandishing Sarah's cigarette lighter that he had admired earlier in the film – and finds herself in the room where the film's climax will take place.

The first thing privileged in this room is an ornate peacock statue made from metal and glass positioned in the foreground, Argento's playful intertextual nod the title of *The Bird with the Crystal Plumage*. Looking around, Suzy finds herself in a shadowy bedroom, and her gaze stops on a bed, its inhabitant disguised by ghost-like curtains draped around it. Again, shadows appear to be another kind of 'broken mirror' where images are distorted: Markos once again appears sleeping in silhouette, just as she did near the sleeping girls after the the maggot infestation. Frightened by Pavlo, Suzy sends the bird ornament crashing onto the floor, waking the shadowy figure. Terrified by the voice speaking to her, Suzy clutches a spiked plume from the now-destroyed bird sculpture and approaches Markos, who mocks her as the room explodes into violence.

Visibly shaken, Suzy is approached by Sarah's knife-wielding, reanimated corpse. But it is the spatial dynamics of this sequence that underscore its narrative and spectacular power, rather than its display of body horror alone. The intuition and confidence in her own intuition that Suzy has developed throughout the film inspires her to attack not Sarah, but the spaced marked on the bed by a flickering, body-shaped ring of light indicating Markos' presence. The moment Suzy stabs the indistinct shape, she converts Markos from pure evil energy into terrifying but ultimately vulnerable flesh. Sarah vanishes and Argento indulges in a series of extreme close-ups as the ornamental spike Suzy has brandished pierces Markos' burnt, scaly body.

With the wicked witch now conquered, as predicted by Professor Milius, the coven can no longer survive and the building itself begins to explode. Symbolically, the first object that we see destroyed is a large, ornate chandelier: the witches have controlled light through the film, and the demise of their power is encapsulated by the privileged destruction of this light source. In one of the film's most beautiful spectacles, the shattering glass and rumbling floors of the Tanzakedemie glitter and swirl around Suzy as she escapes through the crumbling debris. A final glimpse of the school's staff in their death throes is the last thing Suzy sees of the witches, as the walls are slashed and detonated by unseen forces around her. Doors fly off their hinges as she makes her way out of the building, and the toxic yellow windows that line the staircase in the school's foyer explode, revealing the natural hues of the world outside that now stand in contrast to the kaleidoscopic, multi-coloured frenzy the building has embodied.

After a few more spectacular kabooms, Suzy walks free of the Tanzakedemie and the violent supernatural powers that have plagued her throughout the movie. The film makes no bones about this being the ending, and wastes little energy on any kind of normalising, status quo-returning coda. But these final seconds of *Suspiria* show something far more important in an ideological sense: *it allows Suzy to smile*. Drenched in the rain that once tormented her, she beams euphorically as she realises her ordeal over, and that she has changed for the better.

Victory: smiling in the rain

Unlike so many of horror's famous Final Girls, Suzy gives no indication that what lies before her is the trauma of recovery: unlike Laurie Strode (Jamie Lee Curtis) from *Halloween* (John Carpenter, 1978) or Sally Hardesty (Marilyn Burns) in *The Texas Chain Saw Massacre's* (Tobe Hooper, 1974), this Final Girl is in control of her body and her environment, and the knowledge fills her with joy. For all the problematic issues of gender politics that haunt *Suspiria* – from its monstrous witches through to its glamourised displays of violence played out upon young female bodies – it is this moment above all else that grants *Suspiria* an important feminist aspect. Like her fairy tale sisters before her, Suzy's smile promises that she can live happily ever after. It is a future she earned through her strength, her determination, and her understanding and acceptance of her own physicality, a physicality that is proudly both female and feminine.

Text appears on screen: 'You have been watching *Suspiria*.' We need nothing more, and Argento knows it. This textual confirmation is a thundering declaration that positions the entire experience immediately into the past tense. The nightmare is over.

CHAPTER THREE: HELL IS BEHIND THAT DOOR – RECEPTION AND LEGACY

The success of *Suspiria* – both critically and commercially – has become the stuff of legend. In both Italy and abroad, the film is still broadly considered Argento's greatest achievement, and its list of contemporary accolades are seemingly never-ending: it appears regularly in major lists of great cinematic achievements in publications including, *Entertainment Weekly*, *Empire*, *The Village Voice*, and *Total Film*. Over the years, *Suspiria*'s popularity has dwindled little, even though distribution issues plagued it at times as the home entertainment revolution blasted its way into the domestic sphere. As late as 1987, Tim Lucas noted that Key Video – who owned the US rights to the film – still had not released the movie on video, despite being the film that *Video Times* magazine received the most requests for a videotape release.[60] Eventually, *Suspiria* did receive widespread video release around the world, although in some cases it had close brushes with film censors. Most famously, it was included on the UK Department of Public Prosecutions' 'Section 3' list of 80 films it attempted to convict under the Obscene Publication Act that marked the notorious Video Nasties scandal of the mid-1980s. While *Suspiria* was not included in the final list of the 72 films that were ultimately banned, two other Argento titles – *Tenebre* (1982) and *Suspiria*'s sequel, *Inferno* (1980) – were not so lucky.

With advances in media technology, *Suspiria* has remained a constant fascination to both new and old audiences, and has been released on video, laserdisc, DVD and Blu-ray. Cinematographer Luciano Tovoli himself supervised a HD transfer of the film for Blu-ray release in 2010, although he admits 'it is impossible to compare even the best digital master to a film printed with Technicolor's dye-transfer process'.[61] These new releases of *Suspiria* have introduced it to new, appreciative audiences, and the recent rise of Goblin on the international concert circuit – in some cases, providing a live score to *Suspiria*, which they debuted at the Australian Centre for the Moving Image in 2012 to ecstatic Antipodean audiences and have toured internationally ever since – have guaranteed its enduring popularity.

Well over thirty years since its original release, the film's primary promotional image is still Mario De Berardini's iconic original poster art created for the film's initial cinema run. In fact, his black, red and white poster art of the figure of a dancer with a slit throat is one of the most enduring and iconic images of 1970s Italian horror. Working under the professional alias MOS, De Berardinis was a painter who learned the craft under the guidance of famous poster designer Rodolfo Gasparri. During his career, De Berardinis worked with clients including Universal, Columbia, Warner Bros and Dino de Laurentiis, and aside from *Suspiria* he created poster art not only for Argento's earlier *Four Flies on Grey Velvet*, but on a diverse and impressive list of other movies including *Barbarella* (Roger Vadim, 1968), *Slaughterhouse 5* (George Roy Hill, 1972), *Duel* (Steven Spielberg, 1973) and Alan Parker's *Bugsy Malone* (1976).[62]

In Italy, *Suspiria* ranked an impressive seventh place in the year's most successful films,[63] and it also made an impact on foreign markets. According to Barry Forshaw, *Suspiria* 'received good West End exposure'[64] during its initial run in the UK, where even some mainstream reviews admired its bravado: upon its release, Alan Brien at *The Sunday Times* acknowledged it 'invest(ed) every shot with a kind of horrid anticipation of disaster'.[65] The film is also generally regarded as Argento's biggest US hit, despite 20th Century Fox's hesitancy in distributing it. The company even revamped a long-dormant, unused subsidiary called International Classics Inc. to distribute *Suspiria* because of concerns about the impact it might have to its recently boosted industry reputation on the back of the success of George Lucas' *Star Wars*. But if their reasons for doing this were primarily economic, they need not have bothered. According to *Variety*'s Top 50 for the film's eighth week of US release, *Suspiria* reached the Top 5 behind *Star Wars*, Hal Needham's *Smokey and the Bandit*, David Cronenberg's *Rabid* and the James Bond film, *The Spy Who Loved Me*. That week it ranked higher than Martin Scorsese's *New York New York*, schizploitation classic *I Never Promised You a Rose Garden* and Blake Edwards' *Pink Panther Strikes Again* and *Return of the Pink Panther*.[66] According to cinema data analyst Dean Brandum, it took eight weeks to hit this peak because it initially only opened in key cities, and was by this point in saturation release across the country when Fox realised how 'potentially lucrative it could be'. *Suspiria* reported extraordinarily high takings upon its New York opening in particular, taking in what Brandum estimates today would equate approximately to an impressive $351,000 in its opening week in just one theatre. Breaking that figure down, Brandum estimates that approximately 22,500 people saw *Suspiria* in this vital first week at this single New York theatre.[67]

Suspiria's appeal is certainly not limited to Europe or the United States, and the director has often discussed the popularity of his films in Japan. Japanese author and Argento admirer Banana Yoshimoto has noted that the director has 'many enthusiastic fans' in Japan, and that 'there are not many people in my age group that don't know *Suspiria*'.[68] Before he made his sophisticated (and grossly underrated) 1996 rape-revenge film *The Stendhal Syndrome*, Argento was invited to remake Akira Kurosawa's *Yojimbo* (1961), a project eventually helmed by Walter Hill of *The Warriors* fame and released as *Last Man Standing* (1996). There are explicit references to *Suspiria* in the Japanese videogame franchise *Silent Hill*, and his influence there more recently manifests perhaps most visibly in the anime television series *Yurikuma Arashi*. The privileged place of Argento in the Japanese pop cultural imagination was demonstrated in 2013 with the opening of Cambiare, a *Suspiria*-themed bar and grill in Shinjuku's 'Golden Gai' district. *Suspiria* was a major success not only in Japan but also in China, where according to Argento its soundtrack also ranked highly in the music charts.[69]

Yoshimoto is not *Suspiria*'s only literary admirer. Legendary horror novelist Stephen King is a fan of the movie,[70] and experimental writer and feminist icon Kathy Acker's love of the film manifests most explicitly in her 1993 novel *My Mother: Demonology*. Titled 'Clit City', Chapter Three is 'dedicated to Dario Argento, of course'. Here, Acker heads at full-speed into her own visceral, sensual and confronting re-imagining of *Suspiria*, flagged by sub-headings including 'I go back to school', 'The eradication of maggots', 'One murder leads to another', and 'A bat and I become friends'.

My Mother: Demonology is at its most simplistic a literary readymade: she cuts and pastes bits and pieces, and references to Argento lie alongside those to Georges Bataille, Colette Peignot, Emily Brontë, Arthur Rimbaud, Luis Buñuel, Paul Celan, Juan Goytisolo, Radley Metzger, Charles Baudelaire, and even Aerosmith's Steven Tyler. A key figure of literary postmodernism as well as feminism, Acker's influences are worn defiantly on her sleeve, but her writing is simultaneously original and powerful. In a 2002 essay, Diane Fare focused on the relationship between *Suspiria* and Acker's novel, and observed that the raw narrative of Acker's book is far too indistinct to allow any kind of traditional analysis.[71] Like the film itself, the magic lies in its formal construction. Through her reworking of *Suspiria*, Acker's protagonist Cathy/Laure revisits her school years, and they are memories more guided than dictated by Argento's film: she recalls arriving at

Portrait of Kathy Acker © photo credit Michel Delsol

the school when 'the blue and red rain soaked me', and seeing 'rising out of this rain, a building colored red, colored different, from the other edifices'. But Acker ventures well beyond the terrain of mere transcription, and her explicit focus on gender and sexuality are underscored by the variations she introduces to her loose retelling: her Pat hangs on a tampon string, her protagonist has a sexual encounter with the taxi driver, and – most memorably – maggots fall from the protagonist's 'cunt' as well as the ceiling. Even the crucial flower motif is subverted, as the Pat character whispers not 'irises', but 'secret (secrete) pussy'.[72] Acker's affection for Argento's films also led her to inspire the literary work of others: US poet Kevin Killian has said that Acker told him Argento's movies were powerful metaphors for how AIDS worked both in the body of the individual and in society more broadly. Via Acker, Killian found in *Suspiria* a surreality suited to the social and political climate surrounding the disease during the 1980s and 1990s, and this in turn partially inspired his 2001 *Argento Series*.[73]

In Europe, *Suspiria*'s legacy has manifested across the arts in diverse ways. Norwegian thrash/black metal band Susperia are named after the film, but altered the spelling to avoid confusion with groundbreaking 1990s British darkwave band Suspiria. Formed in 1993, the goth duo of Matthew Carl Lucian and Mark Tansley are often erroneously assumed to be named after Argento's film, however Tansley has acknowledged that they were in fact named after a pre-set on his Korg 01W/FD keyboard: 'It was only later we found out about the film, which sort of justified our use of the name'.[74] Fellow British darkwave outfit Miranda Sex Garden released an album called *Suspiria* in 1993, and Austrian goth metal band Darkwell also took their name for their 2000 album from Argento's film.

THE THREE MOTHERS

While the film has doubtlessly made a cultural impact, the legacy of *Suspiria* manifested most immediately in its spawning of Argento's Three Mothers franchise. *Suspiria* was followed by *Inferno* in 1980, and while *Suspiria* focused on Freiburg's Mother Suspiriorum (the Mother of Sighs), its sequel was set in New York and concerned Mater Tenebrarum, the Mother of Darkness. Along with Rome-based Mater Lachrymarum (the titular *Mother of Tears* from the trilogy's final instalment in 2007), *Inferno* provides the basic mythology underpinning the series. In the film's opening moments, we are told that each mother lived in a house built by alchemist and architect E. Varelli, whose voiceover reveals the background to their story. It was only after the completion of the dwellings that he discovered that the sisters sought to dominate the world through their eponymous powers: sorrow, tears and darkness. Varelli provides three keys to revealing the dark secret of the three mothers: firstly is the smell of the locations of each of the three buildings; the second key is hidden in the basement of each residence; and the third and final cryptic clue informs us that it 'can be found under the soles of your shoes'. Much more than *Suspiria*, *Inferno* relies heavily on the broader mythology of the three mothers, linked by their bond as siblings as much as their desire to cause death and destruction on a global level.

Co-financed by *Suspiria* distributor 20th Century Fox, *Inferno* had a budget of $3 million. With this much money riding on it, the project was plagued by studio interference, and Argento has often spoken of the difficulties the production faced. Despite this, it is a movie of which he is notably proud, and it frequently ranks highly in the personal 'best ofs' of many a dedicated Argentophile. After working as 'script consultant' on George A. Romero's 1978 *Dawn of the Dead* (released in Italy and some other international territories as *Zombi*), Argento returned to the directorial role for *Inferno* on the back of the worldwide success of *Suspiria*. Filmed in New York and Rome across 14 weeks in 1979, it starred American actor Irene Miracle, a friend of Bernardo Bertolucci who had recently rose to prominence with her performance in Alan Parker's *Midnight Express* in 1978 (for Italian horror fans, she is most recognisable as one of the two central teenage girls in fellow Italian genre filmmaker Aldo Lado's gloriously vicious *Last House on the Left*-inspired *Night Train Murders* in 1975). Although supposedly conceived with a pre-*Videodrome* James Woods in mind, the role of Mark went to Leigh McClosky, who in 1980 shot to international stardom as Mitch Cooper in the blockbuster soap opera *Dallas*. The inclusion of Sacha Pitoëff as Kazanian is a conscious homage to Alain Resnais' *Last Year at Marienbad* (1961), and both Ania Pieroni (from Fulci's 1981 zombie classic *The House by the Cemetery* and Argento's later 1982 film *Tenebrae*), and Elonora Giorgi (from Paolo Cavara's 1970 giallo *Black Belly of the Tarantula* and Domenico Paolella's 1973 nunsploitation film *Story of a Cloistered Nun*) have close links to Italian genre cinema.

Many of *Suspiria*'s cast returned for *Inferno*, including Alida Valli as caretaker Carol, and Fulvio Mingozzi again as the taxi driver. *Suspiria* co-creator Daria Nicolodi appeared in front of the camera in one of her greatest film performances as Elise Stallone Van Adler. *Suspiria* and *Inferno* diverge in numerous ways, however, not just in terms of their visual styling. Argento wanted it to be immediately distinguishable from its predecessor, and to stand as its own unique creation. The most glaring absence is Goblin, whose soundtrack was so fundamental to the intensity of the first film in the series. For *Inferno*, Argento turned instead to Keith Emerson of Emerson, Lake and Palmer. Argento also enlisted the help of a young William Lustig, who would go on to direct the horror masterpiece *Maniac* later that year, and established the boutique cult and exploitation DVD distribution company Blue Underground in 2002 that released high-quality versions of Argento's films, and the films of many of his Italian genre compatriots such as Luigi Cozzi and Lucio Fulci. Mario Bava's son Lamberto was *Inferno*'s First Assistant Director, and while Mario himself is often incorrectly credited as directing the famous underwater sequence at the beginning of the film (the credit should apparently go to Gianlorenzo Battaglia, who filmed it in a tank in a Rome studio), Bava Sr. assisted on *Inferno*'s special effects.

Despite remaining a fan favourite (famous Argento admirers such as Kim Newman consider it Argento's true masterpiece),[75] *Inferno* was a commercial flop in America. Fox head Sherry Lansing apparently clung in petrified terror to the director himself during a pre-release screening of the film, but it was she who made the decision to not release it theatrically in the United States. With its emphasis on surrealism, even Newman acknowledged her reasoning may have been sound when considering the studio's desire to appeal to a mainstream horror film-going audience.

Daria Nicolodi in
Inferno

The long-awaited final instalment of the Three Mothers trilogy, *The Mother of Tears*, fared no better. Noted as much for its violence – even by Argento's standards it can be considered excessive – the film split critics and fans alike, both groups having long awaited a return to form after disappointing previous efforts such as *Phantom of the Opera* (1998) and *Trauma* (1993) (although 1996's *The Stendhal Syndrome* and 2001's *Sleepless* still remain grossly underrated works in the director's *oeuvre*). *Mother of Tears* saw many of Argento's long-term supporters turn on him, particularly in terms of what some saw as the film's inescapably problematic gender politics: Donna de Ville declared it 'has few redeeming qualities',[76] emphasising it 'is a far more sexualised and seemingly sexist film, misogynistic even, with increased gratuitous female nudity and brutal violence toward female figures'.[77] It fared little better with Argento critic Maitland McDonagh:

> I find *Mother of Tears* sadly unconvincing, from its mundane details (Mater
> Lachrymarum's tacky sacred dress, which looks like a t-shirt decorated with glitter
> pen) to Argento's justification for casting silicon-swollen Israeli model Moran Atias
> as the frequently naked Mother of Tears… Apocalypse Barbie is still Barbie, not the
> embodiment of pure evil.[78]

Relocating the story to Rome and pitting Sarah Mandy (Asia Argento) against the last of the three mothers, the film saw a much-hyped return of Daria Nicolodi to the screen of an Argento film as the overtly intertextual ghost of Mandy's mother. It also saw a welcome return of Udo Kier to the trilogy, and Goblin's Claudio Simonetti provided the soundtrack.

Udo Kier in
Mother of Tears

Filmed in Rome and Turin in 2006, the script for the final instalment of the franchise has a long history. Daria Nicolodi claimed in an interview with *Fangoria* in 1984 that she had a finalised script,[79] while Argento himself announced in late 2003 that he intended to begin shooting the following year. In 2005, US screenwriters Jace Anderson and Adam Gierasch were enlisted by the director to further develop his original treatment. This earlier version of what would eventually become the final script tantalisingly included a role for Max Von Sydow (who had previously appeared in Argento's *giallo Sleepless*) and even Sienna Miller's name was linked to the project at one stage. With a short excerpt premiering at Cannes in 2007, *The Mother of Tears* was released on Halloween in Italy that year, and according to Wikipedia its takings were impressive: it made $827,000 in only two days, reaching $1,917,934 by the end of its first week and it ranked number four at the Italian box office.

BEYOND THE THREE MOTHERS

The legacy of the original *Suspiria* spread well beyond the official Three Mothers series, however. Nicolodi wrote a script with fellow Argento collaborator Luigi Cozzi called *De Profundis* that followed the story of a film crew making a movie about the Third Mother Levana, and the horrors that the diegetically 'real' witch brings to them. Released in 1989 as both *The Black Cat* and *Demons 6: De Profundis* (the latter linking it to another legendary Italian horror franchise), Jones claims the script was Nicolodi's 'setting-the-record-straight take on Levana'. Director Cozzi has emphasised that the film was more a homage to Argento's series (and to Edgar Allan Poe) than a conscious effort to add to it, but despite this the film's fans are few, with Alan Jones dismissing it as a 'spaghetti atrocity'.[80]

Argento returned to the girl's school as the site of horror in *Phenomena* (1985), released in the United States as *Creepers*, where a heavily edited version received widespread distribution on the drive-in circuit. Starring 14-year-old Jennifer Connelly in her first leading role (two years before she would appear alongside David Bowie in the children's fantasy film *Labyrinth* in 1986), while not children as such, the girls in *Phenomena* are notably younger than the cast of *Suspiria*, recalling Argento's initial unfulfilled wish to have his earlier film focus on young children. *Phenomena* cast Connelly as the daughter of a famous American actor who discovers she has psychic abilities while studying at a boarding school in Switzerland. Encouraged by a forensic entomologist friend (played by horror icon Donald Pleasence), she realises she can communicate and control insects, and as the film's Final Girl she uses this skill to unravel a series of violent murders that have plagued the region.

The following year, Argento briefly revisted *Suspiria* in a more unusual manner when he directed 'Action', a promotional television special for Trussardi's 1986 casual wear line. Still quite rare, rumours about this half hour catwalk show have claimed it is effectively a remake of *Suspiria*'s opening sequence, but this is frankly a stretch. While it references Argento's broader *oeuvre* – particularly the iconic black leather gloves of the *giallo* film and a bloodied model beingdragged off stage in a transparent plastic body bag – these references are not really *Suspiria* specific. The *Suspiria* soundtrack is played, however, but even then only briefly. Rather, then-contemporary pop music by artists like Talk Talk and Kate Bush is much more dominant. So although not a restaging of *Suspiria* as such, Argento does reference the film with the inclusion of a simulated rainstorm, allowing glamorous models to frolic in wet, clingy clothes.

With remakes becoming an increasingly common element of the contemporary horror landscape, it is little surprise that a remake of Argento's masterpiece has been rumoured. Dimension Films initially purchased the rights to the film, and in its early stages it had Stephen Katz (who wrote E. Elias Merhige's *Shadow of the Vampire* in 2000) attached to it. The project was ultimately linked to director David Gordon Green of

Pineapple Express fame. Argento has often noted he is no great fan of the idea, and stated in a recent interview that there is ultimately no need for a *Suspiria* remake: 'The film is there. If you want to see it, just put the DVD in.'[81] In 2012 there were reports that Isabelle Fuhrman of *Orphan* (Jaume Collet-Serra, 2009) fame was linked to the film. Green's involvement in the project had been shelved by April 2014, but a year later rumours began circulating about a possible television series being in development. By September 2015, excitement about a *Suspiria* movie remake was reactivated when Italian director Luca Guadagnino announced he was soon to begin filming his re-imagining, starring his regular collaborator Tilda Swinton (who earned her horror stripes in Jim Jarmusch's remarkable 2013 vampire film *Only Lovers Left Alive*).[82]

The initial remake excitement arguably peaked in 2008 when horror website Bloody Disgusting reported a rumour linking American actor Natalie Portman to the project.[83] Portman of course would go onto an Oscar-winning performance as a deranged dancer in another ballet-centric horror film of sorts in Darren Aronfsky's *Black Swan* (2010). While *Suspiria* and *Black Swan* are notably different, their focus on the world of ballet as a site of horror has united them on a basic subgeneric level. There are, however, other 'ballet horror' films that were regularly overlooked in mainstream critical evaluations of *Black Swan*, particularly the beautiful *Étoile* (Peter Del Monte, 1989). Aside from establishing a clear link to Argento through the casting of *Phenomena*'s Jennifer Connelly, *Étoile* also shares significant plot similarities to *Suspiria* as it follows an American dance student who travels to Europe (this time Hungary) to study at a renowned dance school, only to discover that distinctly feminine supernatural forces are working against her.

If *Suspiria*'s legacy required further verification, a 2012 issue of the US *Elle* magazine featured Naya Rivera from the popular television series *Glee* in a fashion shoot recreating the famous image of Suzy in Helena Markos' lair at the end of the film. Argento has been cited as an influence on directors including James Wan, John Landis and John Carpenter, and his legacy is visible in the work of directors like Quentin Tarantino, Martin Scorsese and Brian De Palma. Pascal Laugier's notorious French horror film *Martyrs* (2008) is dedicated to Argento, and *Suspiria* was famously namedropped in the smug indie comedy *Juno* (Jason Reitman, 2007). Along with a range of other Italian horror films from the period (particually *gialli*), *Suspiria* is a visible influence on Belgian directors Hélène Cattet and Bruno Forzania's *Amer* (2009) and *The Strange Colour of Your Body's Tears* (2013).

Of all the recent horror films to wear *Suspiria*'s imprint, however, *Another* (Jason Bognacki, 2014) and *Livid* (Julien Maury and Alexandre Bustillo, 2011) most sincerely extend its spirit. *Livid* is a dramatic shift from the French duo's previous maternal slasher *Inside* (*À l'intérieur*, 2007), but like its predecessor it shares Argento's fundamental fascination with sensory impact. The film is built around the mysterious figure of Deborah Jessel (a nod to Henry James' 1898 novella *The Turn of the Screw*), a now elderly and incapacitated woman requiring the care of the film's protagonist, Lucy (Chloé Coulloud). Lucy discovers that Jessel was once a ballet teacher, and inside her large gothic mansion Lucy finds gruesome, life-size figures of a young ballerina. Lucy's investigation reveals Mrs Jessel's past as a kind of vampire witch: the film explicitly links her to *Suspiria* with the inclusion of a certificate that shows Mrs Jessel studied at the Freiburg Tanzakademie.[84]

Livid (Julien Maury and Alexandre Bustillo, 2011)

More recently, Jason Bognacki's *Another* acknowledges Argento in its end credits, and the legacy of *Suspiria* manifests in this remarkable low-budget masterpiece in a number of ways. Even placing its central story about two monstrous witch sisters – both with a significant maternal link to the film's protagonist, Jordan (Paulie Rojas) – aside, *Another* shares *Suspiria*'s love of the hallucinatory, the vivid and the shocking on a near-primal level. As Anton Bitel has noted: '*Another* turns out not to be the *Suspiria* rip-off that horror fans have been dreading, but a dynamic reimagining better than anything in their wildest dreams.'[85]

While the legacy of *Suspiria* – and Argento's wider *oeuvre* – is broad, Bognacki adopts more than just its formal strategy in his formal strategy in how he goes about creating his own equally hypnotic cinematic universe. *Suspiria*'s enduring importance therefore stems from the challenge it issues to other artists to take risks, to be daring, to be audacious. As cinematographer Luciano Tovoli observed in the lengthy interview that concludes this book,

> I like films that are surprising and provocative, that take risks with their visual solutions, and that might be judged as the fruit of 'bad taste'. I hate successful films that travel on an easy wave of 'good taste': for me, that is simply anti-culture.

'The legacy of *Suspiria* is a kind of admonishment,' he continues. 'Without revolt and a sense of refusal, we cannot advance the evolution of film language and creativity in general.' Argento makes these demands of of fellow artists and audiences alike, and it is precisely this spirit of defiance that makes watching *Suspiria* such an intoxicating and unforgettable experience. As film theorist and academic Patricia MacCormack so elegantly notes in one of the DVD extras of the stunning 2010 Cine-Excess release of the film:

> *Suspiria* is one of the most radical horror films that has ever been made, and the precise reason for this is that it is unapologetic in the way it expresses horror and the way it demands the opening up of the viewer to take pleasure in things that they cannot describe.

Suspiria's exquisite terror stems from the dark beauty of losing control. It champions the chaos of the senses over the rationality of the intellect. Ilt demands that we let light, sound and colour move us. *Suspiria* is a carnival, a dance, a poem, and above all else, a glorious deathblow to the assumed supremacy of logic and reason.

APPENDIX: AN INTERVIEW WITH *SUSPIRIA* CINEMATOGRAPHER, LUCIANO TOVOLI (2014)

I was very moved by something you said in an interview with Alan Jones that I would like to ask you about. In this interview, you are talking about some personal tests you did for Dario Argento to see if he was interested in your ideas before you committed to working on *Suspiria*. You said, 'Dario saw what I had done, went up and physically touched the screen and said it was fantastic'. This is a very powerful image to me – the idea of Argento touching the light that you had made! This is how I feel when I watch *Suspiria* even today, that I do not just see it with my eyes but I can touch it: its visuals appeal to all my senses. It is a very poetic movie in this regard. Is this a response you get a lot to the film? Was this 'poetry' of light a deliberate choice on your part?

First of all, in the years before (but still close to) *Suspiria* I was starting to become tired and bored of the naturalistic use of colour and light that we all used then, myself and the others. I remember when I was just out of film school in Rome at the end of the fifties with my late friend Néstor Almendros we made a strong and almost sacred commitment in front of a glass of good red Tuscan wine to respect and reproduce in all our films forever natural, available and realistic light. Suddenly, when almost twenty years later Argento proposed to me this film - not exactly and simply an horror film, as we can discuss later - I had the sensation that another world, another horizon had opened up in front of my eyes. It was a much freer horizon, with more fresh air than just the straightforward reproduction of the real world allowed. This was a world of creative freedom, finally unchained from the obsession with realism. But it did not happen just like that. In his previous films, the light in Argento's films was perfect because it was not so noticeable. In (Vittorio) Storaro's one (*The Bird with the Crystal Plumage*, 1970), the film relied on light and colour but in the estetic way that would have made Vittorio so celebrated around the world later. From my side, I had already by that time worked with Michelangelo Antonioni who taught me a new expression that changed my thinking about film and colour, the concept of 'colour dramaturgy'. This meant that in film, not only are the characters and plot important, but film being a visual art means that colour is also an element of fundamental and dramatic importance. I tried to apply this formula, and *Suspiria* came out of it almost naturally.

In my first meeting with Dario and his father (Salvatore Argento, *Suspiria*'s producer), I came out with a crazy proposal that ever since then I have liked to use, although it did leave a negative impression on the producer! I asked Dario innocently if it would have been possible during shooting to just launch bucketfulls of body paint of different colours onto the face of the actors, primary contrasting colours like red, blue and green. Argento's father called for a time-out in the meeting, and took Dario into another room. He said to him very simply, 'this guy is crazy. Let's go get him out of my office immediately!' Of course, I made my screen tests without launching liquid paint onto the actors' faces, but I did illuminate them with huge lights that were placed very close to them, filtered through heavy, coloured velvets. My use of these velvet screens made me very popular on the spot, but also had a negative side, too. Maybe from these kinds of Modernist inspirations - or out of normal methods of lighting - came the physical side of the film that calls to be touched like Dario did when I showed to him my early Technicolour tests

When you have spoken about what has inspired your work in *Suspiria*, you have often talked about artists like Mondrian, Edward Hopper, Jackson Pollock and Leonardo Da Vinci. These artistic influences are very apparent in the film's painterly qualities. We often talk about film as 'moving pictures', but in the case of *Suspiria* I think this is even more true. This love of great art is something that you and Dario Argento obviously share – can you tell me how much of your work together (on *Suspiria* and on later projects you did together) was discussed in terms of fine art?

I did not speak so much with Dario about this, despite him being passionate about painting: it is difficult not to be when you are born in Rome, especially in regards to Classical and contemporary masters. Personally, many of these influences I only discovered retrospecitvely years later looking maybe at an old scratched copy of the film in a little theatre in Paris or New York. I was astonished that I was not aware at the time of shooting how much I had soaked my hands in a deep passion for contemporary masters. Of the Classics that form the foundations of my visual cultural literacy, I prefer not to say anything because I have already often been accused of pretentiousness in my expressions and I do not want to aggravate the situation! Suffice to say that I am a photographer, and like any serious photographer I rationally search for creative inspiration from directly inside the open field of photography. I'm totally convinced that photography does not need to imitate the classical arts to fully express itself. But I am also an art lover in all its forms, and I cannot force my mind to not run in the infinite prairies of the unconsciousness, bringing to the surfaces emotions given by painting, literature, sculpture and music: it is not worth searching for an explanation for this. The fact is simply that *Suspiria* is certainly the result of all these contaminations. It has been around for some 37 years, and apparently it is not ready to vanish into oblivion like many other films that I have made.

One of the best descriptions I have heard about the colour and light in *Suspiria* is a comparison a few critics have made who describe it as looking like a stained glass window (for example, in the scene where Suzy is in the taxi). How do you feel about this description?

Inside the taxi is one of my favourite close-ups from my entire career, and I have to say in general too. We shot this magical close-up in studio back in Rome almost at the end of production. I was striving to continue roughly what I had already utilized for the Munich airport scene, where I put coloured gels everywhere (several pilots in command of landing planes called the control tower enquiring about all these strange, hyper-coloured lights that did not correspond to any of their aeronautical codes! They did not know that it was the *Suspiria* code!). Once in the studio, I had the idea of carefully replicating the exterior lights and colours from Munich, where I also coloured the rain in green and red, scared as I was that the artificial rain would appear far too realistic! For this close-up inside the car, I pushed the idea of pure colours mixing with one another even further, letting my imagination go freely. I finally arrived at an idea of a changing and moving stained glass window. I asked my crew to build two wide cylinders around ten feet in diameter outside the car, with small openings covered by coloured gels and different grades of frost. By turning the cylinders in the opposite direction to each other with a single fixed Fresnel light inside of each them, the magic was created! Dario and I were as fascinated with the results then as we are still today.

I understand that you used mirrors a lot in *Suspiria* to help you get very sharp images.

This leads me to ask you about my favourite scene in the film, where a maid (Franca Scagnetti) reflects a bright flash of light into Suzy's face with a shard-like silver utensil. This is a very beautiful, powerful scene and I have no idea how you would have captured that incredible moment – can you tell me more about this technique and your approach?

Working with the famous French director and screenwriter Francis Veber after *Suspiria*, he told me once that when you have an idea, it is like finding a steel nail, and you must beat this nail obsessively. Almost all of *Suspiria* was made with a sense of this urgency, to push different nails in as deeply as I came to do. Mirrors were one of my 'nails' in *Suspiria*. At this time, I hated all the classical studio lights, and I searched for a way to build around the camera a kind of forest that contradicted the rationality of a classical studio lighting disposition. The more impenetrable the forest of cables, lights, flags, and frames of velours were tightly encircling the camera, the more that the light that came out from this bunch of almost inextricable knots seemed to me (and probably was) geometrically ordered, and pure in colour. It was as if in my mind I had staged the drama of these ideas, searching to liberate themselves from the chains of the chaos of our passions. What those around me probably noticed, however, was the fact that I was a kind of excessively invasive cinematographer and I have been accused of that for years! The only one that observed my work with amusement, often giving the decisive input, was naturally Dario who inspired all the visions of *Suspiria*: not suggesting or commanding anything too precisely, but feeding my hungry mind with all the necessary elements to be able to respond with such extremes. Under his inspired and confident artistic sensibilities and his specific experience, he gave a lot of freedom to his collaborators, intervening only when he perceived that we were lost for a moment, bringing us back on the right path. *Suspiria* is of course mainly his film: it is the result of all his impressive cultural and cinematic knowledge, and his immense talent. I was like a child playing with this gigantic toy, totally unaware of the consequences of my playfulness. Dario at all times drove the boat into safe waters, guided by his incredibly precise and brilliant vision of the film.

Another scene I love very much is where Suzy and Sarah are swimming. Was this scene difficult to shoot? (It reminds me of a similar scene from Jacques Tourneur's *Cat People*)

The difficult part for that scene was building a very wide bridge at the borders of the swimming pool so that the camera was suspended over the water surface at the height of the faces of the actresses. I needed to maintain the same frame as they were advancing through the water. For once, the light was natural light (although there was some diffusion on their faces). I will see *Cat People* – I have never seen it!

Can you tell me a bit more about the mood on set? You have said in previous interviews that it was not relaxing as such, but there was a shared mood of being part of something very creative and new. Can you tell me more about this?

The mood on the set of *Suspiria* was the usual one for a film where the director is striving to realize his dream and does not want to hear the word 'impossible'! Argento gave us the time, and all we needed to experiment in new ways. Of course, I have made many films where the mood was almost excessively relaxed, but for me the shooting of these films was already in the basket, and a waste of time and money. Normally with Dario Argento there are not very many fights or discussions. He knows what to expect from his collaborators, and they know that they have to give him their maximum effort. The deal was clear from the beginning, and it was very transparent and honest. But of course, neither one of us were stupid enough at the time to believe we were doing something tremendously unique and important, we would have felt totally ridiculous. We worked seriously, in a pleasant and civilized way, but not exactly a totally relaxed mood. But how could shooting in that atmosphere be relaxed? Every moment a new problem to be solved would rise up, on every shooting day, just as in every other film!

You have mentioned that your favourite lighting effect in the film was how the use of mirrors allowed you to get such deep, rich blacks in the final scene, but still brought out the bright lustre of the golds. Some of the film's most powerful scenes happen in these very dark – almost completely black – environments, with dramatic flashes of colour.

I very often utilized mirrors in a way where beams of reflected light were very close and absolutely parallel to the walls and decorations in a way that I brought out the colours and the smallest details of the set in an almost 3D-like manner. I carefully searched for a way to separate the light that fell on the actors from the light that was on the set. This distinction gave me the same freedom that I could have got with the then blue (today green) screen technique, but I was doing it directly on set with no post-production. This was the precise request I'd made to Argento before we began shooting: every image has to be built entirely on stage, and not one single frame can go through a post-production process. For example, the killing of Helena Markos was realized through a semi-transparent mirror placed at a 90-degree angle in front of the lens in a way that the image on Jessica was shot directly, while the image of Helena lit her more dimly against the black background. This was one of several techniques utilized in the past, and in the film there is a lot of classical (and from today's digital perspective, kind of naïve) special effects.

I understand you were not interested in horror films until you worked with Argento, but of course you have gone on to work with him again on both *Tenebre* (1982) and of course more recently *Dracula 3D* (2012).

It is true that before meeting Argento I was as ignorant of horror films as today I am ignorant about so many other subjects! But I realized well before I met him that he was a powerful director, capable of drawing enthusiastic audiences to the theater. One summer Sunday afternoon I heard noise down in the street, and looking out the window I saw a large group of people: one group were going in one direction, and another moving in the opposite direction. I knew later that in these two theaters so close to my apartment, the same Argento's film was showing: both theaters were full, so those who could not get into one were hoping to find a place in the second but both were full with people standing even in the corridors. With that much chaos, my immediate thought was, 'If this director can generate all this turmoil in the audiences, his films have to be something very special'. I then began to see all the previous Argento film that I had not seen before.

You speak very beautifully about Jessica Harper's face in your interview with *American Cinematographer* in 2010, and in *Suspiria*, there are lots of different kinds of faces (young, old, male, female). Can you tell me about some of your memories of lighting and filming these different types of faces?

Our planet has provided the most beautiful and ever changing natural landscapes in the form of mountains, oceans, forests and deserts. Human beings remain astonished by these variegated marvels of nature, sculptured similarly on our faces through deep emotions. For that I like to make a 180-turn of my eyes away from these natural landscapes, and instead discover that humans offer the most interesting landscapes of all: these faces moved by natural, marvellous spectacles. Plains, mountains and oceans are all represented in the human face, with a range of refined variation that compete with the immensely spectacular representations that nature offers us on a gigantic scale. A few inches of a tridimensional epidemic surface can express a thousand notes, related to a thousand emotions. As a photographer first and later as a cinematographer, these facial landscapes are the ones I prefer. Having had the privilege to place bright lights and deep shadows, and to play with colour on faces like Jessica Harper and Alida Valli (just to name two of the several I met while making *Suspiria*) is one of the motivations that continues to inspire my work ever since.

The scene outside the BMW building where Suzy meets Dr Mandel and Professor Milius is very different to anything else in the film: at first, it recalls your previous background with more naturalistic lighting, but as the conversation about witches becomes stranger, the images start to play tricks on us with reflections collapsing into each other! It almost feels like a little joke you are playing with yourself – it starts off very 'rational' but then becomes more and more 'surreal'.

Sometimes reality can play a role in an abstract film through contrast. In the middle of this scene, I deliberately altered reality with reflections that opened up the imagination on a subliminal level. Each film has a very precise visual architecture, and this design in the mind of a cinematographer is the real fundamental value that drives everything! Technique? Old or new technologies? These are not too significant to me, just the consciousness that the possibilities of film have been abandoned well before their natural expiration date. Money? Yes. Market and a worldwide marketing campaign? Yes. But these have nothing to do with the evolution of a real film language. Yesterday we had film and digital post-production! A brief golden era of film that quickly vanished. But for me, the real golden era of film was the time of Technicolour and Kodak: without these two giant contributors, it would not have been possible to have had *Suspiria*.

You have described the driving aesthetic behind *Suspiria* as 'never to subtract, but to add'.

I was taught in high school that one of the secrets of creativity is to search to eliminate unessential elements from a busy reality, and through this process of elimination to discover the essence of reality itself. One of the more impressive demonstrations of this canonic principle responds to the name of Michelangelo: he declared very openly that to sculpt his masterpieces, it was a matter of eliminating all the parts that hid the already existing and very clearly designed statue that lay inside the block of Carrara's marble (the Tuscan mountains from where he bought to Rome this special marble). He was kind of eliminating the 'packaging', and discovered inside the marble dust a hidden gift! But this packaging resisted its elimination, and through this fight came all the immense and eternal beauty of Michelangelo's creations.

We can put these two elements together on the table before us and play a little bit: I am the smallest of ants in the field of the arts in comparison to the pure, absolute and universal essence of creativity that I consider Michelangelo (he is well above all other human artists in history). I have to say very humbly that in this little film called *Suspiria*, I tried to apply the opposite principle. The package box with a white screen at one side (the physical house of our 'frames'!) was not an empty package that I had to be eliminated and destroyed, but instead filled with whatever element I considered essential. Being that the film was shot in colour, I considered colours as structural, dramaturgic elements and not just other decorative appendix (under the influence of one of my masters with whom I collaborated, Michelangelo Antonioni): visual elements that supported this little 'insignificant' film artefact. I say 'insignificant' in proportions versus the work of my unique hero Michelangelo, the sculptor and painter of course, but apparently this fight between colours has been quite significant considering the many, many people that still venture to see it. These are people who appreciate it without apparently any temporal delay, and even today the dynamic fight of its colours drives the story like an *inarrestabile* wave.

You once described *Suspiria* as a gothic fairytale, can you expand on this?

Naturally some of these references have been identified in the film long after *Suspiria* was shot, often by chance. For example, I saw the 1928 Jean Epstein film, *The Fall of the House of Usher* and I liked it very much, and recognized some lightning techniques we used in *Suspiria* in it (but ours were coloured). Same with the Mario Bava's masterpiece *The Demon's Mask*, (aka *Black Sunday*, 1960), where this great artist was in charge of direction, cinematography and special effects, achieving often astonishing results with minimal means. He made Barbara Steele an iconic, international star. In *Interview with a Vampire*, the work of my colleague Philippe Rousselot (who I admire a lot) visually interpreted that story in a way that is totally opposite to *Suspiria*, and is quite absurd to suggest that this style could be separated from the film itself! He visually interpreted the story of Neil Jordan's film with total mastery.

With *Suspiria* now one of the most famous and beloved horror films ever made, its influence is to be seen across a large number of horror films from all over the world.

A Swedish journalist once brought me his ponderous academic research, a study he had made on all the commercials, films and stills that he believed had been influenced by *Suspiria*. Hundreds, in his opinion! This seemed like kind of an exaggeration to me. Unfortunately I have lost this record, but I have to say that I do not lose sleep trying to remember this list of imitators. The only colleague who in all my long career ever came to me and admitted that he literally copied a scene from one of my films was my late friend Néstor Almendros, who in *Kramer versus Kramer* utilized a lighting idea I had in Marco Ferreri's film *The Last Woman* for the child's bedroom. But Almendros was my friend ever since we were at film school in Rome, and I take that as an homage from one friend to another!

I understand you have worked on the HD transfer of the film for a Blu-ray release. From a technical perspective, what are the strengths and weaknesses of Blu-ray – for you, can it capture the same qualities of celluloid?

Sorry, but nothing can capture the same quality of 'celluloid' as you call it, especially if the image base is not celluloid but a less inflammable material. Why? Because one is a physical image created by materials as colours - or dark or grey little grains in the B&W films - traversed by a beam of natural or artificial light. This is what happens when a coloured window is traversed by a beam of sunlight: it is simply physical. The reactions that happen in the developing machine that are impossible to visualize without the risk of ruining the image are also physical, chemical, dynamic reactions. These things have to do with temperature and time in the sense that the time it takes to develop a film can change the quality of the image, as does the temperature. All these are physical reactions, interacting when you merge film and chemicals.

I do not see any similarities with the digital process. The Blu-ray – as all the other previous systems – are series of numbers and mathematical combinations, and the image that comes out is often the result of an intricate calculation process that demands this algorithmic abstract concert to try to produce the same end result as the 'celluloid images': this is simply demanding the impossible, and why? Again, the first is a physical image; the second is a mathematical image. How they could ever be the same? But the real problem is that we have all been so enthusiastic about the changes in technology, but very few have analyzed the processes needed in order to be be more creative with it. With these new tools all over the world, in general we are letting pass the idea that anyone can make films with much less money than it used to cost, and that anyone with their first camera they bought in the videocamera shop in the street under their apartment can become by magic an Argento or a Fellini or an Antonioni. The film profession suffers a lot for this absolutely false idea, but unfortunately it is a winning, poisonous idea and there's nothing to do about that!

Another director you have worked with many times is Barbet Schroeder, who makes very different films from Dario Argento! Can you tell me about your work with Schroeder?

Barbet Schroeder and I are a real team, and we will remain a tight team until our twelfth film! Until this number is reached, I will simply continue to do all Schroeder's films. We have a very serious exclusivity pact, a kind of a deal without papers or signatures - it is our friendly pact. We have just finished our seventh film together, so we have another five to accomplish before we can possibly break the pact. Schroeder is such a close friend that I could write a full book about his professional and human qualities, and for that reason I would prefer not to make comparisons with other directors who I also consider very highly.

Speaking of other collaborations, two of your most famous shots involve very long takes (I am thinking of the last scene of Antonioni's *The Passenger* and the crane shot over the house in Argento's *Tenebre*). How would you say that your work with Antonioni in particular influenced later work, particularly that with Dario Argento?

It is a fact – and, in a way, it was fate – that I was a young cinematographer having the occasion to work with one of most celebrated film directors in the world, who of course not only influenced my later work but also influenced my whole life. For about twelve years I was at his side, and I received daily lessons from a master who never acted like a master giving lessons! It was as if he was almost secretly making his movies almost secretly and you had to capture the elements of his unique lessons.

Who could ask for more? At the same time, I am perfectly aware that looking at things from another perspective, I could have immediately become a cinematographer distinguished for Antonioni's visual style, powerful and perfectly modern. This would have been very easy for me to do, and probably would have made me quite successful too! But instead, I searched continuously - as I am still doing today – for my personal style in the faces of different and such expressive actors, under the often precise instructions of so many different directors, in the interesting new ways to light sets, and in the fascination and mystery of a perfectly composed line from a script. I like to swim freely across of all these essential film components, like a long-distance swimmer who uses their (his) arms, legs, and whole body to make their (his) way through the waves of the open ocean. This has been, is and definitely will continue to be my way of searching for my own style style, a search that never I will consider accomplished.

What do you see as *Suspiria*'s most important legacy?

The legacy of *Suspiria* is a kind of admonishment. Without revolt and a sense of refusal, we cannot advance the evolution of film language and creativity in general: to revolt against all the comfortable habits that permeate our minds that forbid us to take risks, and to refuse any kind of easiness has been always my risky recipe. Easy solutions are there all the time within a hands reach, and difficult but creative solutions are well hidden. You need time to find them, and time is money: producers normally do not like you to spend time searching for original solutions. For this, you have to close your ears to solicitations to go faster and keep searching and searching (trying, of course, not to get fired!). What can save you is the *quality* of what you show on screen. This is the best safeguard of all! To make a movie is a quite complicated process, and a risky one - very often for the producer or the director or an actor as much as it is for the cinematographer. Why lose the opportunity to break traditions, and unconsciously condemn ourselves to the level of mediocrity? The task takes too much energy to *not* to try and play the match fully until the last second! I like films that are surprising and provocative, that take risks with their visual solutions, and that might be judged as the fruit of 'bad taste'. I hate successful films that travel on an easy wave of 'good taste': for me, that is simply anti-culture.

NOTES

1. Joe Bob Briggs, 'One of the Scariest Flicks in Splatter History'. *San Francisco Examiner-Chronicle*, 1 October 1989. p. 27.

2. Kim Newman, *Nightmare Movies*. London: Bloomsbury, 2010. p. 142.

3. Steve Biodrowski, 'Interview: Dario Argento Sheds the Mother of All Tears', *Cinefantastique*, 30 April 2008. http://cinefantastiqueonline.com/2008/04/interview-dario-argento-sheds-the-mother-of-tears/

4. Disney's *Snow White and the Seven Dwarfs* has a number of directorial attributions, including Larry Morey, Wilfred Jackson, Ben Sharpsteen, Perce Pearce, David Hand, and William Cottrell.

5. J. Hoberman, 'Suspiria Shock: Two Runs in Two Weeks', *The Village Voice*, 1 September 2009. www.villagevoice.com/2009-09-01/film/suspiria-shock-two-runs-in-two-weeks/

6. Tom Gunning, 'The Cinema of Attraction[s]: Early Film, Its Spectator and the Avant-Garde'. *The Cinema of Attractions Reloaded*. Ed. Wanda Stauven. Amsterdam: Amsterdam University Press, 2006. p. 382.

7. Alan Jones, *Profondo Rosso: The Man, the Myths and The Magic*. FAB Press: Godalming, 2004. p. 94.

8. See: Laura U. Marks, *The Skin of the Film: Intercultural Cinema, Embodiment, and the Senses* (Durham: Duke University Press, 2000) and *Touch: Sensuous Theory and Multisensory Media* (Minneapolis: University of Minnesota Press, 2002).

9. Noel Carroll, *The Philosophy of Horror or, Parodoxes of the Heart*. New York: Routledge, 1990. p. 24.

10. Alan Jones, 'Argento' *Cinefantastique* 13.6/14.1 (1983): p. 20.

11. I write about *The Stendhal Syndrome* in my 2011 book *Rape-Revenge Films: A Critical Study* (Jefferson: McFarland, 2011) and the article 'The Violation of Representation: Art, Argento and the Rape-Revenge Film', *Forum: University of Edinburgh Postgraduate Journal of Culture and the Arts*, 13 (Autumn 2011).

12. Email to author.

13. Alan Jones (2004), p. 90.

14. Ibid., p. 91.

15. James Gracey, *Dario Argento*. Harpenden: Kamera Books , 2010. p. 19.

16. Ibid., p. 20

17. See: Xavier Mendik , 'From the Monstrous Mother to the 'Third' Sex: Female Abjection in the Films of Dario Argento' in *Necronomicon: The Journal of Horror and Erotic Cinema: Book Two*, London: Creation Books, 1998. p. 112-3; Donna de Ville, 'Menopausal Monsters and Sexual Transgression in Argento's Art Horror'. *Cinema Inferno: Celluloid Explosions from the Cultural Margins*. In Robert G. Weiner and John Cline (eds). Plymouth: Scarecrow Press, 2010. p. 63.

18. Luca M. Palamerini, and Gaetano Mistretta, *Spaghetti Nightmares: Italian Fantasy-Horror As Seen Through the Eyes of their Protagonists*. Key West: Fantasma Books, 1996. p. 17.

19. Alan Jones, *Profondo Rosso: The Man, the Myths and The Magic*. FAB Press: Godalming, 2004. p. 15.

20. Ibid., p. 16.

21. Ariston Anderson, 'Horror Master Dario Argento on Fear and Happiness (Q&A)', *The Hollywood Reporter*, 6 August 2014. www.hollywoodreporter.com/news/horror-master-dario-argento-fear-723085

22. Maitland McDonagh, *Broken Mirrors, Broken Minds: The Dark Dreams of Dario Argento*. Minneapolis: University of Minnesota Press, 2010. p. 62.

23. Alan Jones (2004), p. 81.

24. See: Adrian Horrocks, '*Suspiria*: Magic is Everywhere'. *Necronomicon: The Journal of Horror and Erotic Cinema. Book Four*. Ed. Andy Black. Hereford: Noir Publishing, 2001. p. 33; de Ville, Donna. 'Menopausal Monsters and Sexual Transgression in Argento's Art Horror'. *Cinema Inferno: Celluloid Explosions from the Cultural Margins*. In Robert G. Weiner and John Cline (eds). Plymouth: Scarecrow Press, 2010. p. 64.

25. See: Xavier Mendik (1988), p. 122; Howard Hughes, *Cinema Italiano: The Complete Guide from Classics to Cult*. London: I.B. Tauris & Co Ltd, 2011. p. 240.

26. Maitland McDonagh, p. 240.

27. Stephen Daultrey and Monica Esposito, 'Dario Argento Interview' *Bizarre*, November 2009. http://www.bizarremag.com/film-and-music/interviews/8317/dario_argento.html

28. Alan Jones (2004), p. 69.

29. Ibid., p. 60-1.

30. See: Howard Hughes, p. 242.

31. Although first published in 1821, there were six editions issued between 1822 and 1853, with an expanded version in 1856 that almost doubled the length of the 1821 version.

32. Rei Terada, 'Living a Ruined Life: De Quincey Beyond the Worst', *European Romantic Review*, 20. 2 (April 2009). p. 177.

33. Noel Carroll, *The Philosophy of Horror or, Paradoxes of the Heart*. New York: Routledge, 1990. p. 16.

34. Michael Mann, 'Asia and Dario Argento'. *Ion Magazine*. 23 October 2007 http://www.ionmagazine.ca/culture/film/asia-dario-argento

35. Stephen Thomson, '*Suspiria*: Possessed Bodies and Deadly Pointe', *Electric Sheep Magazine*, 1 February 2010 http://www.electricsheepmagazine.co.uk/features/2010/02/01/suspiria-possessed-bodies-and-deadly-pointe/

36. Stanley Manders, 'Terror in Technicolor'. *American Cinematographer*. February 2010. p. 68-76.

37. Alan Brien, 'Suspiria', *The Sunday Times* (UK), 9 October 1977 (n.p)

38. Alan Jones (2004), p. 86.

39. See: Alan Brein. n.p.

40. Alex Fitch, 'Interview with Dario Argento', *Electric Sheep Magazine* 3 July 2009 http://www.electricsheepmagazine.co.uk/features/2009/07/03/interview-with-dario-argento/

41. Stanley Manders, p. 69

42. Stephen Thrower, 'Suspiria', in *Art of Darkness: The Cinema of Dario Argento*. Ed. Chris Gallant. Godalming: FAB Press, 2001. p. 129.

43. Luca M. Palamerini, and Gaetano Mistretta, p. 16.

44. Howard Hughes, p. 243.

45. Alan Jones, *Profondo Rosso: The Man, the Myths and The Magic*. FAB Press: Godalming, 2004. p. 13.

46. James Gracey, *Dario Argento*. Harpenden: Kamera, 2010. p. 112.

47. Horrocks, Adrian. '*Suspiria*: Magic is Everywhere'. *Necronomicon: The Journal of Horror and Erotic Cinema. Book Four*. Ed. Andy Black. Hereford: Noir Publishing, 2001. p. 48.

48. Alan Jones (2004), p. 94.

49. Ibid., p. 14.

50. James Gracey, p. 94.

51. Stephen Thrower, 'Suspiria', in *Art of Darkness: The Cinema of Dario Argento*. Ed. Chris Gallant. Godalming: FAB Press, 2001. p. 137.

52. Xavier Mendik. 'Suspiria'. *100 Cult Films*. Eds. Ernest Mathjis and Xavier Mendik. BFI/Palgrave Macmillan: London, 2011. p. 191.

53. Alan Brien, 'Suspiria', *The Sunday Times* (UK), 9 October 1977 (n.p)

54. Email to author.

55. James Gracey, p. 93-94.

56. Adrian Horrocks, '*Suspiria*: Magic is Everywhere'. *Necronomicon: The Journal of Horror and Erotic Cinema. Book Four*. Ed. Andy Black. Hereford: Noir Publishing, 2001. p. 47.

57. Linda Schulte-Sasse, 'The 'Mother' of All Horror Movies: Dario Argento's *Suspiria* (1977)'. *Kinoeye: New Perspectives on European Film*. 2.11 (10 June 2002) http://www.kinoeye.org/02/11/schultesasse11.php

58. Email to author.

59. Email to author.

60. Tim Lucas, 'The Butchering of Argento', *Fangoria* #66 August 1987. p. 15.

61. Manders, Stanley. 'Terror in Technicolor'. *American Cinematographer*. February 2010. p. 75.

62. De Berardinis' daughter Valérie has curated a Flickr gallery of her father's work that is worth a visit https://www.flickr.com/photos/mos-deberardinis/sets/72157616995566675/

63. Howard Hughes, *Cinema Italiano: The Complete Guide from Classics to Cult*. London: I.B. Tauris & Co Ltd, 2011. p. 243.

64. Barry Forshaw, *Italian Cinema: Arthouse to Exploitation*. Harpenden: Pocket Essentials, 2006. p. 93

65. Alan Brien, 'Suspiria', *The Sunday Times* (UK), 9 October 1977 (n.p)

66. '50 Top-Grossing Films (Week Ending September 21)', *Variety* 28 September 1977. p.12.

67. Email to author.

68. Email to author.

69. Steve Biodrowski, 'Interview: Dario Argento Sheds the Mother of All Tears', *Cinefantastique*,

30 April 2008. http://cinefantastiqueonline.com/2008/04/interview-dario-argento-sheds-the-mother-of-tears/

70. Luca M. Palamerini and Gaetano Mistretta, *Spaghetti Nightmares: Italian Fantasy-Horror As Seen Through the Eyes of their Protagonists*. Key West: Fantasma Books, 1996. p. 18.

71. Diane Fare, 'A Spectacle of Pain: Confronting Horror in Kathy Acker's My Mother: Demonology', *European Journal of American Culture*, 21.2 (2002), p. 98-111.

72. Kathy Acker, *My Mother: Demonology*. Ne York: Grove Press, 1993.

73. Tony Leuzzi, 'An Interview with Kevin Killian', *Eeoagh: A Journal of the Arts*, 5 (February 2009). http://chax.org/eoagh/issuefive/killian.html

74. Email to author.

75. Kim Newman, *Nightmare Movies*. London: Bloomsbury, 2010. p. 146.

76. Donna de Ville, 'Menopausal Monsters and Sexual Transgression in Argento's Art Horror', *Cinema Inferno: Celluloid Explosions from the Cultural Margins*. In Robert G. Weiner and John Cline (eds). Plymouth: Scarecrow Press, 2010. p. 71.

77. Ibid., p. 68.

78. Maitland McDonagh, *Broken Mirrors, Broken Minds: The Dark Dreams of Dario Argento*. Minneapolis: University of Minnesota Press, 2010. p. xxv.

79. See: 'Interview with Dario Argento and Daria Nicolodi Taken from FANGORIA Magazine, Volume No. 35 Issue 4' http://web.archive.org/web/20050306220246/ http://argento.vervost.de/argento/interview_inferno.html. From the *Master of Colors Dario Argento* website. Archived on 28 May 2006 from the original which was here: http://www.argento.vervost.de/argento/interview_inferno.html

80. Alan Jones, *Profondo Rosso: The Man, the Myths and The Magic*. FAB Press: Godalming, 2004. p. 52.

81. Ryan Gilbey, 'Why Dario Argento Thinks the Gory Scenes of a Movie Are 'The Most Important Parts'', *New Statesman*, 8 November 2013. www.newstatesman.com/film/2013/11/why-dario-argento-thinks-gory-scenes-movies-are-most-important-parts

82. Fred Topel, 'Joe: David Gordon Green on Nicolas Cage, Suspiria and Little House on the Prairie', *Crave Online* 10 April 2014. www.craveonline.com.au/film/interviews/673569-joe-david-gordon-green-on-nicolas-cage-suspiria-and-little-house-on-the-prairie

83. Brad Miska, 'Update #2: Update #2: Natalie Portman to Topline Suspiria Remake!' *Bloody Disgusting*, 6 August 2008. http://bloody-disgusting.com/news/13203/

84. Many thanks to James Gracey for pointing this out: I missed this vital document on my first viewing of the film.

85. Anton Bitel, 'FrightFest 2014: Another Review', *FilmLand Empire*, 27 August 2014. www.filmlandempire.com/2014/08/frightfest-2014-another-review.html

BIBLIOGRAPHY

Acker, Kathy. *My Mother: Demonology*. New York: Grove Press, 1993.

Anderson, Ariston. 'Horror Master Dario Argento on Fear and Happiness (Q&A)', *The Hollywood Reporter*, 6 August 2014. www.hollywoodreporter.com/news/horror-master-dario-argento-fear-723085

Barber, Chris. 'Discovering the Esoteric Argento.' *Eyeball: The European Sex and Horror Review* 3.3 (Summer 1992), p. 4-5.

Biodrowski, Steve. 'Interview: Dario Argento Sheds the Mother of All Tears', *Cinefantastique*, 30 April 2008. http://cinefantastiqueonline.com/2008/04/interview-dario-argento-sheds-the-mother-of-tears/

Brien, Alan. '*Suspiria*', *The Sunday Times* (UK), 9 October 1977 (n.p)

Briggs, Joe Bob. 'One of the Scariest Flicks in Splatter History'. *San Francisco Examiner-Chronicle*, 1 October 1989. p. 27.

Carroll, Noël. *The Philosophy of Horror or, Paradoxes of the Heart*. New York: Routledge, 1990.

Crawford, Travis. 'Argento on Stendhal: The Maestro of Mayhem Discusses His Newest Film The Stendhal Syndrome', *European Trash Cinema*, 15 (1997), p. 25-31.

Daultrey, Stephen and Monica Esposito, 'Dario Argento Interview' *Bizarre*, November 2009. http://www.bizarremag.com/film-and-music/interviews/8317/dario_argento.html

de Ville, Donna. 'Menopausal Monsters and Sexual Transgression in Argento's Art Horror'. *Cinema Inferno: Celluloid Explosions from the Cultural Margins*. In Robert G. Weiner and John Cline (eds). Plymouth: Scarecrow Press, 2010. p. 53-75

Fitch, Alex. 'Interview with Dario Argento', *Electric Sheep Magazine* 3 July 2009 http://www.electricsheepmagazine.co.uk/features/2009/07/03/interview-with-dario-argento/

Forshaw, Barry. *Italian Cinema: Arthouse to Exploitation*. Harpenden: Pocket Essentials, 2006.

Gallant, Chris (ed). *Art of Darkness: The Cinema of Dario Argento*. Ed. Chris Gallant. Godalming: FAB Press, 2001.

Gilbey, Ryan. 'Why Dario Argento Thinks the Gory Scenes of a Movie Are 'The Most Important Parts", *New Statesman*, 8 November 2013.

Gracey, James. *Dario Argento*. Harpenden: Kamera Books, 2010.

Guins, Ray. 'Tortured Looks: Dario Argento and Visual Displeasure'. *Necronomicon: The Journal of Horror and Erotic Cinema*. Book One. Ed. Andy Black. London: Creation Books, 1996. p. 141-153.

Hoberman, J. '*Suspiria* Shock: Two Runs in Two Weeks', *The Village Voice*, 1 September 2009. www.villagevoice.com/2009-09-01/film/*suspiria*-shock-two-runs-in-two-weeks/

Horrocks, Adrian. '*Suspiria*: Magic is Everywhere'. *Necronomicon: The Journal of Horror and Erotic Cinema*. Book Four. Ed. Andy Black. Hereford: Noir Publishing, 2001. p. 33-51.

Hughes, Howard. *Cinema Italiano: The Complete Guide from Classics to Cult*. London: I.B. Tauris & Co Ltd, 2011.

Jones, Alan. 'Argento' *Cinefantastique* 13.6/14.1 (1983): p. 20-21

Jones, Alan. *Profondo Rosso: The Man, the Myths and The Magic*. FAB Press: Godalming, 2004

Lucas, Tim. 'The Butchering of Argento', *Fangoria* #66 August 1987. p. 14-17, 65.

Manders, Stanley. 'Terror in Technicolor', *American Cinematographer*. February 2010. p. 68-76.

Mann, Michael. 'Asia and Dario Argento'. *Ion Magazine*. 23 October 2007 http://www.ionmagazine.ca/culture/film/asia-dario-argento

Martin, John. 'What You See is What You Don't Get, or 'I Wanna Know About the Mystery Dance'. *Fantasy Film Memory*. 4/5 (1991). p. 1-10.

McDonagh, Maitland. *Broken Mirrors, Broken Minds: The Dark Dreams of Dario Argento*. Minneapolis: University of Minnesota Press, 2010.

Mendik, Xavier. 'From the Monstrous Mother to the 'Third' Sex: Female Abjection in the Films of Dario Argento' in *Necronomicon: The Journal of Horror and Erotic Cinema: Book Two*, London: Creation Books, 1998. p. 110-133.

Mendik, Xavier. 'Suspiria'. *100 Cult Films*. Eds. Ernest Mathjis and Xavier Mendik. BFI/ Palgrave Macmillan: London, 2011. p. 191-3.

Mitchell, Tony. 'Prog Rock, the Horror Film and Sonic Excess: Dario Argento, Morricone and Goblin'. *Terror Tracks: Music, Sound and Horror Cinema*. Philip Hayward (ed.). London: Equinox Publishing, 2009. p. 88-100.

Newman, Kim. *Nightmare Movies*. London: Bloomsbury, 2010.

Olney, Ian. *Eurohorror: Classic European Horror Cinema in Contemporary American Culture*. Bloomington: Indiana University Press, 2013.

Palamerini, Luca M. and Gaetano Mistretta, *Spaghetti Nightmares: Italian Fantasy-Horror As Seen Through the Eyes of their Protagonists*. Key West: Fantasma Books, 1996.

Schulte-Sasse, Linda. 'The 'Mother' of All Horror Movies: Dario Argento's *Suspiria* (1977)'. *Kinoeye: New Perspectives on European Film*. 2.11 (10 June 2002) http://www.kinoeye. org/02/11/schultesasse11.php

Thomson, Stephen. '*Suspiria*: Possessed Bodies and Deadly Pointe', *Electric Sheep Magazine*, 1 February 2010 http://www.electricsheepmagazine.co.uk/ features/2010/02/01/suspiria-possessed-bodies-and-deadly-pointe/

Thrower, Stephen. '*Suspiria*', in *Art of Darkness: The Cinema of Dario Argento*. Ed. Chris Gallant. Godalming: FAB Press, 2001. p. 126-144.

DEVIL'S ADVOCATES

"Auteur Publishing's new Devil's Advocates critiques on individual titles offer bracingly fresh perspectives from passionate writers. The series will perfectly complement the BFI archive volumes." Christopher Fowler, Independent on Sunday

THE CURSE OF FRANKENSTEIN – MARCUS K. HARMES

"Harmes definitively establishes the decades-long impact of The Curse of Frankenstein on the gothic horror film genre."
Sydney Morning Herald

WITCHFINDER GENERAL – IAN COOPER

"I enjoyed it very much; it sets out all the various influences, both before and after the film, and indeed the essence of the film itself, very well indeed." Jonathan Rigby, author of English Gothic

THE DESCENT – JAMES MARRIOTT

"James Marriott makes a strong case for [The Descent] being the finest example of the films that revitalised the genre in the early years of the new millennium..." Black Static

BLACK SUNDAY – MARTYN CONTERIO

"Throughout, Conterio's approach, while immensely in-depth, is conversational in tone and very accessible... this monograph is an invaluable read for anyone with an interest, not only in Bava's work, but in the history of Italian horror cinema. Essential." Exquisite Terror

Printed and bound by CPI Group (UK) Ltd, Croydon, CR0 4YY

13/04/2025

14656604-0001